About the author

David Chandler is professor of international relations and research director of the Centre for the Study of Democracy, University of Westminster. He is the author of several books and edits the journal *Resilience: International Policies, Practices and Discourses.*

FREEDOM VERSUS NECESSITY IN INTERNATIONAL RELATIONS

HUMAN-CENTRED APPROACHES TO SECURITY AND DEVELOPMENT

David Chandler

Zed Books

LONDON | NEW YORK

Freedom versus Necessity in International Relations: Human-centred Approaches to Security and Development was first published in 2013 by Zed Books Ltd, 7 Cynthia Street, London N1 9JF, UK and Room 400, 175 Fifth Avenue, New York, NY 10010, USA

www.zedbooks.co.uk

Copyright © David Chandler 2013

The right of David Chandler to be identified as the author of this work has been asserted by him in accordance with the Copyright, Designs and Patents Act, 1988

Set in Monotype Plantin and FFKievit by Ewan Smith, London
Index: ed.emery@thefreeuniversity.net
Cover designed by www.rawshock.co.uk
Printed and bound in Great Britain by CPI Group (UK) Ltd, Croydon, CRO 4YY

Distributed in the USA exclusively by Palgrave Macmillan, a division of St Martin's Press, LLC, 175 Fifth Avenue, New York, NY 10010, USA

All rights reserved. No part of this publication may be reproduced, stored in a retrieval system or transmitted in any form or by any means, electronic, mechanical, photocopying or otherwise, without the prior permission of Zed Books Ltd.

A catalogue record for this book is available from the British Library
Library of Congress Cataloging in Publication Data available

ISBN 978 1 78032 484 5 hb
ISBN 978 1 78032 483 8 pb

CONTENTS

ACKNOWLEDGEMENTS

This book would not have been possible without the stimulating working environment provided to me over many years by the Centre for the Study of Democracy and the Department of Politics and International Relations at the University of Westminster. In addition, I would like to thank Naeem Inayatullah, who provided an initiating insight; Jonathan Joseph and Michele Ledda, for their comments on the draft; Ken Barlow and the team at Zed Books; and the two people I have gained from most, through discussions and disagreements in the course of preparing and writing this book, Julian Reid and Paulina Tambakaki.

Parts of this book draw on recently published or forthcoming material as well as conference papers and lecture presentations. Chapter 2 reworks material from a number of invited lecture presentations, including: the paper 'From the external world to the inner world: rethinking "human-centred" or "agent-centred" understandings of development and conflict', prepared for a workshop at the University of Geneva, in April 2011; 'Rethinking the human subject', presented at the workshop 'Contemporary debates in political studies' at Makere University, Uganda, in May 2011; and the lecture 'Rethinking the human subject', at the University of Coimbra, Portugal, in September 2011. Chapter 3 is based upon work developed in the paper 'Insecure subjects: vulnerability, empowerment and resilience', prepared for 'Vulnerability: a symposium', University of Otago, Dunedin, New Zealand, in November 2010; 'The rise of resilience: rethinking agency and governance interventions', a seminar presentation at the University of St Andrews, in April 2011; and the paper 'International statebuilding and the inculcation of resilience', presented at the workshop 'Resilient futures: the politics of preventive security', at the University of Warwick, in June 2011. It also draws from material in the forthcoming article in the journal *International Political Sociology*, 'Resilience and the autotelic subject: towards a critique of the societalization of security'.

Chapter 4 draws on material from the paper 'Where is the human in human-centered approaches to development? A Foucauldian critique of Amartya Sen's "Development as freedom"', presented at the symposium 'Reading Michel Foucault in the postcolonial present', University of Bologna, Italy, in March 2011, and the paper '"Human-centred" development? Rethinking "freedom" and "agency" in international development', presented at Cambridge University, in May 2012. Chapter 5 is based on material prepared for the workshop 'Interrogating the use of norms in international relations', organized by the International Political Sociology Working Group at the International Studies Association convention, Montreal, Canada, in March 2011, and the forthcoming article in the journal *Democratization*, 'Promoting democratic norms? Social constructivism and the "subjective" limits to liberalism'.

Chapter 6 draws from the paper 'Beyond intervention? Post-interventionist framings of international relations', prepared for the international conference, 'Interventionism in international relations today', l'Université Libre de Bruxelles (ULB), Brussels, in June 2011; 'The rise of post-intervention', presented at the conference, 'Politics in the global age: critical reflections on sovereignty, citizenship, territory and nationalism', at the Indian Institute of Technology Madras, Chennai, India, in December 2011; and material in the published article 'Resilience and human security: the post-interventionist paradigm', *Security Dialogue*, 43(3) (2012). Chapter 7 is an amended version of the paper 'Our morals and theirs: politics beyond the biopolitical subject', presented at the international symposium, 'Politics beyond the biopolitical subject', Griffith University, Brisbane, Australia, in December 2011. I would, of course, like to thank all those involved in generously inviting, hosting and funding these opportunities to discuss and develop the work presented in this book, particularly the generous support of the Finnish Academy funded research project 'Governing life globally: the biopolitics of development and security', led by Professor Julian Reid at the University of Lapland.

'At first we call particular acts good and evil without consideration of their motives ... Then we assign the goodness or evil to the motives ... We go even further and cease to give to the particular motive the predicate good or evil, but give it rather to the whole nature of man; the motive grows out of him as a plant grows out of the earth. So we make man responsible for the effects of his actions, then for his actions, then for his motives and finally for his nature. Ultimately we discover that his nature cannot be responsible either, in that it is itself an inevitable consequence, an outgrowth of the elements and influences of past and present things; that is, man cannot be made responsible for anything, neither for his nature, nor his motives, nor his actions, nor the effects of his actions.'

Nietzsche, aphorism 39, *Human, All Too Human*

1 | INTRODUCTION: THE SUBJECT OF GOVERNANCE

Introduction

This book intends to break new ground in analysing the consequences of conceiving the world in human- or agent-centred terms. While placing the human agent or actor at the centre of the world is often understood to be progressive and empowering, this is very far from the case. Human-centred approaches start with the individual or community, often conceived as vulnerable and insecure, and consider ways in which individuals and communities can become empowered or capacity-built in order to have the agency to better cope with, withstand or challenge the vicissitudes of our global and complex world. This book makes the simple point that focusing on the inculcation of individual and community agency, ethical reflectivity or resilience, as a way of addressing problems of insecurity, conflict or development, tends to see the human subject as the problem, rather than the material social and economic relations within which it is embedded. In fact, once human agency is seen as the level at which problems can be resolved, material and structural constraints fade into the background or are seen as merely a product of poor behavioural choices. The focus on the differential subjective or cognitive aspects of human agency, and their social and cultural institutional constraints, in this way has replaced the rationalist understanding of the universal subject operating in specific social, economic and political circumstances.

The declaration that we are 'humans', radically proclaimed as if it were some new discovery, is a call for the recognition that the problems of the world need to be understood in the context of our richness and diversity: in the fact that we are emotional, social and complex beings, embedded in a world which is continually subject to change. This sounds like an empowering and radical shift, especially when discursively posed in contradistinction to a neoliberal rational-choice understanding of humans as rational calculators of self-interest with no normative considerations for others (Thaler and Sunstein 2008: 7).

Yet the trope of the natural, rational or autonomous individual has been a subject of critique at least since Karl Marx's powerful indictment of the Robinson Crusoe figure of classical political economy for naturalizing the social relations of the market in *Capital*, Volume 1 (1954: 81). The difference between Marx's time and today, of course, is that Marx wanted to extend the sphere of human freedom by revealing the coercive constraints of the structuring social relations operating beneath the surface of free market appearances. Today the purpose is entirely the opposite; instead we are told that it is our 'human' qualities, our distinct social, emotional and cognitive flaws and fallibilities, which explain why our freedoms need to be carefully managed and why our choice-making necessitates facilitative and empowering governance intervention.

Of course, it could be argued that an analytical focus on human agency and choice-making possibilities holds out the promise of social transformation, whereas the focus on historical, social, economic and structural constraints acts to rationalize or legitimize inequalities and differences. In fact, it is increasingly held that placing analytical emphasis on structural constraints limits the space for human agency and restricts the subjective choices available, thereby constraining possibilities for progress. This book seeks to argue the opposite: that, in fact, human-centred approaches to the problems of insecurity, conflict and development close down the possibilities for human freedom. Human-centred approaches limit the possibilities of social transformation because the problems are located in the behaviour and decisions of those considered to be the most vulnerable or insecure. The focus on empowering and capacity- and capability-building individuals and communities held to be 'at risk' emphasizes their need to develop, change or adapt to enable them to cope with, to survive, or to thrive in the world. The world as it exists is understood to be open to change and transformation, but increasingly this transformation is seen to be centred on human practices and understanding. In this way, the human becomes the determinant focus rather than the external world beyond the subject. Increasingly, rather than focusing on the problems of the external world, the inner world of the subject becomes the focus for aspirations of social transformation.

In this framework, rather than freeing the human subject, the freedom of the human subject is understood as the problem rather than the solution. In a world seen to be complex, globalized and lacking the laws and regularities that enabled instrumental, goal-directed policy-making and political aspirations, linear or teleological understandings of human progress are no longer deemed possible. Without modernist understandings of space and time, structuring and giving meaning to contingency, human freedom of choice-making apparently needs to be subordinated to the world through the inculcation of adaptive learning and ethical responsibility. In the subordination of the human to the world it appears, counter-intuitively, that we have a surfeit of freedom; our dominant discourses and interpretations of the world tell us that we have more freedom than ever before.

In our globalized world we are often told that, even without any political struggle or any wish to be free, we are increasingly responsible for the choices that we make. Governments are increasingly stating that they can no longer rule us in the old ways; that we, as citizens, are much too aware and reflective to passively accept advice or direction. Apparently we have access to so much information, are so diverse in our preferences and have so many opportunities, that they can no longer treat us as passive or obedient subjects, being instructed or told what to do.[1] We are also told that giving citizens greater responsibility provides a check on possible abuses of state power; more and more areas of life are becoming democratized as power and authority diffuse down to the level of the individual.[2]

We have so much freedom, in part, because we lack the previous constraints of inherited tradition or bureaucratic state regulation. We are regularly informed that we have been freed by the collapse of traditional frameworks of values and that we have demanded and voted for the end of paternalistic state interventions in our education and welfare. We now have to take responsibility for our decisions and choices. This is nowhere more the case than in terms of our increasing awareness of our freedom of choice in terms of our personal or private lives – in our lifestyle choices – where we are now aware that the decisions we make about how much we exercise, whether to smoke, what we eat and how we parent can have a major influence on our own lives and those of other people. In a world in which it appears that choice is all around us, it may seem paradoxical to argue that our freedom is, in fact, becoming the central problematic around which understandings and practices of governance are shaped.

The key point that is developed in this book is that choice-making does not equate to freedom today. The philosophical and political history of liberal modernity was one that revolved around the construction of the liberal subject as an autonomous, rational actor, capable of making choices that were in the interests both of the individual and of the society as a whole. The freedom of choice-making enabled the constitution of the subject, understood to be universal and entitled to equality at the ballot box and under the law. It was through our free choice-making – from the mythical construction of the social contract, founding the state of liberal modernity, through to the choice-making of elections, legitimizing government rule, and of the market, revealing our preferences and interests – that the liberal world was both constructed and legitimized. It is impossible to imagine the liberal world without the free – autonomous – rational, choice-making subject at the centre of it.

This book will argue that today we still have the legacy of a liberal world – a world of choice-making subjects – but that we no longer understand the human subject as the rational and autonomous choice-making subject of liberal modernity. Instead we are understood to be socially embedded subjects, within limiting institutional and cognitive frameworks – inherited from the past and shaped by hierarchical and problematic social relations and socio-environmental norms and constructs. While we are increasingly aware of the lack of universal rationality of the subject, the external world is also held to have changed or to need a different and non-linear framework of understanding in which rationalist approaches, which presuppose an external world of law and regularity, can no longer guide our policy-making.

It appears that our assumption of the 'naturalness' of the universal rational subject, supposing that autonomy is positive (rather than needing to be carefully nurtured and managed – and therefore potentially problematic), has been the greatest error of liberal modernity. In fact, the world appears to be full of problems caused by precisely this liberal or neoliberal lack of attention to the shaping of the frameworks through which our 'freedoms' can be safely exercised. Once autonomous choice-making is problematized, human freedom is transformed from a universal starting assumption of liberalism to a policy goal of managing and capacity-building the subject. Choice-making is increasingly viewed as problematic today precisely because we are not understood to be either rational or autonomous subjects. Our freedom is considered through a discourse of limits as we become aware that we are not somehow separate from the world but live as choice-making subjects which are entirely embedded within the world around us: both as beings who produce this world and as beings who are produced by it.

In this understanding of our embeddedness, our freedom as subjects is constrained both from above and from below. From above, we are not free because we live in a world increasingly understood to be globalized: a world whose problems can be traced back to our actions or decisions, however small or minor. If the common trope that 'when a butterfly flaps its wings in one part of the world it can cause a hurricane in another part of the world' is true, then it is clear that a globalized world makes us responsible for the supposed distant effects of our decisions and actions because, even without intention, we are *causing* effects in the world. Our increasing consciousness of the fact that even the most minor actions or choices we make in the world have consequences that we can now process-trace – as a method of inferring a causal mechanism (see, for example, Bennett and George 1997) back to our actions – necessarily restricts our freedom of decision-making. In the globalized world, without external laws and regularities, human subjects still exist as agents but lose their capacity to be subjects capable of acting to transform their external circumstances though conscious intention.

From below, our freedom of choice is also limited, again by a process-based understanding of what was previously understood as a series of separate and discrete acts. If the world demonstrates the problematic nature of human choices, then we increasingly believe that liberal assumptions of the autonomous and rational subject can no longer hold. We are perceived to be unable or incapable of making decisions or acting in our own interests or in society's greater good. If we were rational subjects, we are told, surely we would save for our retirement, exercise, not smoke, etc. Increasingly, the choice-making subject is understood as bounded by its social context, its thought processes, life experiences, values, beliefs, environment and a myriad other factors. Rather than having a universal capacity for rational or non-problematic choice-making, we are understood to be universally poor actors and decision-makers, each bounded in our actions and decision-making in different ways. These limitations cause us to act and choose poorly. What we imagine to be freedom of choice is actually just an expression of very limited understanding of the *causes* of our actions.

Complex, overlapping and interlinking processes are understood to create chains of *causation* that remove the meaningfulness of contingency: which remove free choice-making. Once we understand the world as globalized, in the sense of being made up of causal relations that do not work through fixed structures of meaning, we can no longer act as subjects in the world. Projects of external transformation – of transforming ourselves through work in and through the world – depend on fixed structures of meaning; whether these are natural laws or laws of capitalism or other forms of social and economic relations. It is through these fixed structures of meaning that we understand ourselves as able to master necessity – the relations of cause and effect. It is only through mastering necessity that we are capable of producing our own freedom. Human freedom, in effect, is (or was) the story of the growth of science and knowledge enabling humans to master the world in which they lived: the story of the transformation of necessity into freedom. As we shall consider in this book, freedom of choice stems from the meaningful contingency of the world – the structured gap between our actions and their final ends – which provides room for experimentation and learning. We are capable of exercising our freedom only when we can conceive ourselves as acting meaningfully in the world – i.e. in relation to temporal and spatial structures – as subjects, capable of adapting our actions and decisions towards our chosen goals.

In today's world, we are held to have learnt, precisely through the growth of science and technology, that the story of the teleology of human freedom is a mythical and, in fact, a dangerous one. We are told that relations of necessity, relations of causation exist, but that they can never be mastered. These laws of causation are too complex to be grasped in the simple mechanistic terms of incremental or linear cause and effect. Process-thinking (also termed 'resilience thinking', Walker and Salt 2006) understands the world in terms of dynamic complexity. The world is so complex – so full of unknowable and uncontrollable necessities – that modernist views of laws of social relations or laws of nature or traditional understandings of government control and regulation make little sense. In this world, human actions and choice-making become the one fixed point which appears to be amenable to conscious human intervention. How to act on this fixed point then becomes the key problematic, informed by process-tracing – working backwards from what are perceived as problematic actions. We then attempt to alter or address the causes of these actions, through shaping the cognitive and societal environments in which these behavioural choices are made.

As the freedom of decision-making ebbs away from our understanding of the world, the problems of the world become reproduced as the problem of human cognitive capacities and increasingly articulated as the problem of the human subject itself: not amenable to any easy remedy or solution. While the problematic of liberalism relied on a positive rationalist view of human choice-making, human-centred understandings rely on the problematization of human choice-making in order to rationalize a very different framework of governance. This is not government, in liberal terms, legitimized and limited by the sphere of human freedom but its opposite. Human-centred governance is legitimized by the recognition of the problem of freedom and autonomy, by the need to extend governance into spheres that were previously understood to be outside of the realm of liberal government. In making freedom, individual choice-making, the problematic at the heart of governance understandings, human-centred frameworks assert themselves as the rule of necessity against the realm of freedom.

After liberalism

This book is about the transition beyond liberal forms of rule and how this shift is reflected in dominant understandings of freedom and intervention, constructed through discourses of agent-centred or human-centred frameworks of capacity-building and empowerment. It will be suggested that what we understood to be the victory of liberalism with the end of the Cold War in 1989 can now be more fully appreciated as the beginning of the problematization of traditional liberal assumptions about the role of government in relation to social problems and the management of the economy. The rethinking of these relations was already set in chain from the late 1970s onwards, in the period dominated by neoliberal thinking, understood as part of a project of social contestation involving the curbing of trade union power and the rolling back of the state, pushing responsibility for social welfare on to society rather than the state. As many theorists and commentators have powerfully described, neoliberalism's shift of emphasis from the state to society took a variety of forms in different national and international contexts, but all have rhetorically appealed to calls for human freedom and choice-making independence and been hostile to the alleged limiting of freedom by the paternalism of big-government provision of services and of top-down interventionist policy provision (see, for example, Harvey 2005).

In exploring the shift of policy emphasis from state to society, analysts of neoliberalism often emphasized and criticized this as responding to the needs of capitalism and big business but neglected to critique the ways in which the liberal project was understood in much more limited terms in relation to freedom – particularly the ways in which the role of government was being transformed as states were seen to lose their freedom to shape the societies which they governed. The neoliberal period understood states as heavily bureaucratized barriers to the unleashing of social capacities through the mechanism of market forces. The introduction of the market into areas previously highly regulated was understood as emancipating social potential which otherwise would be dormant – held back by the heavy-handed top-down regulation of society by the interventionist state. This shift towards a societal understanding of unleashing the immanent dynamic of the market reflected the disillusionment with state-led attempts at development, highlighted by the stagnancy and eventual collapse of the Soviet system and the economic crises of the early and mid-1970s with the end of the post-war boom, which created the social conditions under which trade union power, welfare benefits and professional privileges could be rolled back. As Hannah Arendt among others presciently noted, the early discourses of 'freedom' within neoliberalism already constituted a substantial critique of state interventionist, Keynesian approaches in which public policy-making had a central role in directing economic and social processes (Arendt 1998, 2005). The 'freedoms' of the market are freedoms of the private or social sphere, not those of the public or political sphere, as the possibilities for policy choice at the level of government are heavily limited.

For many Marx-inspired theorists, such as David Harvey, neoliberalism was mainly seen as an economic phenomenon, driven by the needs of capital accumulation. The interpretation often given is one of the victory of capitalist class power as the resistance of more state-interventionist approaches to welfare and security was incrementally dismantled. In which case, the shift to societal understandings, of social or individualized sufficiency, is a straightforward one, depending on the traditional or classical liberal understanding of the subject as universally rational and autonomous. In fact, these assumptions are the source of Harvey's critique: that precisely because of the false subject of liberalism, the freedoms of the market clash with the demands of social justice (and that the left has failed to critique neoliberalism on these grounds):

> Asymmetric power relations tend ... to increase rather than diminish over time unless the state steps in to counteract them. The neo-liberal presupposition of perfect information and a level playing field for competition appears as either innocently utopian or a deliberate obfuscation of processes that will lead to the concentration of wealth and, therefore, the restoration of class power. (Harvey 2005: 68)

Harvey's left critique of neoliberalism is therefore based upon the clash between the subject as understood in and through neoliberal discourses, as rational and autonomous, and the real, sociological, socially embedded subject, which lacks the capacities and capabilities and rationalities required to compete under capitalism as if it were a 'level playing field'. Once neoliberal discourse is recognized as a 'failed utopian rhetoric masking a successful project for the restoration of ruling-class power' then 'mass movements voicing egalitarian political demands and seeking economic justice, fair trade, and greater economic security' can potentially re-emerge (ibid.: 203–4). Here, the subject being constructed through neoliberal discourses is understood as the classical liberal subject, and it is through the critique of this 'utopian' subject that neoliberal discourse can be exposed as the ideological expression of ruling-class hegemony.

Other theorists, often taking their inspiration from Foucault, rather than Marx,[3] have also staked out highly influential interpretations of the neoliberal paradigm at the heart of the shift from states as responsible for addressing the problems of society to understanding society itself as both the source and solution of these problems. For these commentators, the primary focus was not that of critiquing neoliberalism, as driven primarily by economic needs, but rather of looking at how new mechanisms of regulation operated and were put into effect. Their focus was on the subject being constructed under liberal and neoliberal discourses. The precondition of neoliberal discourse appeared to be the acceptance of the autonomous, rational subject, making possible the rolling back of the state on the basis

transformative political projects and instead argue that the global and complex world demands changes in human agency and choice-making. We retrospectively learn which decisions are good or bad and should seek accordingly to preventively or proactively inculcate the capacities and capabilities that will enable us to make better or more reflective choices in the future.[5]

In the chapters which follow, the key theme that will be drawn out is that the discourse of understanding the rule of necessity, and the focus on the agency and empowerment of marginal subjects, is less a project of the management of rule through freedom (whether in the cause of capitalist accumulation or liberal governmentalism) than a framework which rearticulates the limits of human progress as those of human agency itself.

Overview of the book

In the chapters which follow, I will draw out further the relationships between the understanding of necessity as external imposition and the internalization of the capacities for transformation of the human subject. I particularly wish to do this through the analytical exposition of our understanding of freedom and societal intervention in the human-centred problematic, through which we intervene in the cause of human security, human development and human freedom.

Chapter 2 introduces the shifting relationship between freedom and necessity, expanding upon the thematic briefly touched upon above. The focus of the chapter is that the relationship between freedom and necessity cannot be understood in the purely objective terms of technological and scientific progress. How we construct the relationship between freedom and necessity is highly dependent upon how we understand ourselves as embedded in communities that enable us to construct a world of laws – demarcating a sphere of freedom, through which we can pursue our goals through a process of learning and development, both individually and collectively. Without meaningful forms of structuring our engagement with the external world, we lose the freedom of the goal-determining subject as we lose the capacity to articulate our actions within a process over which we have direction and responsibility.

Chapter 3 introduces the problematic of resilience. In discourses of resilience there is a clear assumption that governments need to assume a more proactive engagement with society. This proactive engagement is understood to be preventive, not in the sense of preventing future disaster or catastrophe but of preventing the disruptive or destabilizing effects of such an event. In this sense, the key to security programmes of resilience is the ability of citizens to respond to or adapt to security crises. The subject or agent of security thereby shifts from the state to society and to the individuals constitutive of it. In many ways, this shift away from a sovereign-based understanding to a societal understanding of security, under the guidance of resilience, could be understood as a deliberalizing discourse, one which divests security responsibilities from the level of the state down to the level of the citizen. This chapter considers some of the genealogical aspects of discourses of resilience as a human-centred, societal or individualized understanding of security (particularly focusing on the work of Friedrich von Hayek and Anthony Giddens) in order to work through some of the consequences of the state's divestment of security responsibilities for classical liberal framings of freedom and autonomy. It thereby seeks to draw out the illiberal restrictions on individual freedom that are concomitant with resilience discourses of societal security.

Chapter 4 focuses on the agent-centred understanding of capacity-building in relation to human freedom. In today's dominant conceptualization of human-centred approaches to development, human agency has been placed at the centre and is increasingly seen to be the measure of development, in terms of individual adaptive capacities and capabilities. The individualized understanding of development removes the mediating understanding of contingency. There is no gap between the individual and the world. The individual is in the world but without any social relations mediating the actions and choices of the individual and the effects of these choices and actions as they appear in the world. This view of the individual as the creator of the world – of the individual as responsible for the world – can start the analysis of the world only from the individual subject itself. In this analysis, the world becomes entirely a construct of the agential actions and choices of the individual, and therefore it is termed an 'agent-centred' or 'agent-orientated view' (Sen 1999: 11). This chapter therefore critically engages with the view of human action and choice-making as constitutive of the world and of the problematic understanding of human agency which must necessarily be articulated within this approach.

Chapter 5 analyses the discursive construction of difference in terms of the continuum of vulnerability. The increasing dominance of necessity over freedom and the agential production of necessity can be clearly seen in the shifting frameworks in which change has been understood in the international sphere. This chapter charts the problematization of agency and the construction of problems in terms of vulnerable subjects and analyses how this shift has been reflected in our understandings of the barriers to change, through three conceptually distinct and chronologically distinguishable stages: the early 1990s view that liberal transformation would be universalized with the Cold War victory of liberal ideals and the spread of new global norms of good governance; the mid- to late-1990s view that barriers to the promotion of social and economic transformation could be understood as the product of state or elite self-interests; and the human-centred perspective, dominant since the 2000s, that the promotion of security and development necessarily involves much deeper and more extensive external intervention in order to 'free' the subject through first transforming social institutions and societal practices. Through charting the shifts in the understanding of international norms of governance, this chapter seeks to highlight the problems inherent in agent-centred discourses of understanding that emphasize the importance of subjective agency, normative choices and cultural and ideational frameworks of understanding.

Chapter 6 analyses the reformulation of societal intervention in terms of empowering or capacity-building the vulnerable subject. In liberal discourses of international relations, international intervention was understood as undermining sovereign rights. In a world constructed in the legal and political framework of rights subjects, intervention and sovereignty were conceptual opposites: intervention denoted the denial of freedom and autonomy. This chapter is concerned with the shifting understanding of intervention under regimes of human-centred governance. In this framing, the world is no longer constructed on the liberal basis of rights subjects but sociologically, around subjects understood to lack capacities and capabilities and therefore to be in need of empowerment. Discourses of intervention as empowerment operate on a different register to liberal discourses and are seen to operate at the societal (domestic) level rather than the (international) political or legal level. In particular, discourses of human security are analysed to highlight that it is within this sphere of discussion that the shift to the societal level has enabled discussions of international intervention to go beyond the disputed conceptions of humanitarian intervention and the 'responsibility to protect' in liberal constructions of the 1990s.

Chapter 7 analyses the possibility of going beyond human-centred frameworks of understanding. The post-liberal project lacks its own self-generated dynamic, merely reflecting the exhaustion of the emancipatory impulse of the liberal project. However, as Arendt presciently warns (2005: 190), the seemingly natural and uncontested removal of the external world, as the unlimited field for the expansion of human freedom, has its own laws of consequence, impacting on all areas of our subjective experience of ourselves as actors in the world. The potentially devastating effects of this shift to the internal world of the subject will be drawn out here. Perhaps we are not yet truly at home in the internalized, human-centred, world (without the world): perhaps we are not yet the resilient subjects of the human-centred imaginary. Perhaps merely because we cannot help being human subjects a (different) world is indeed possible (ibid.: 201). In the closing chapter, I suggest ways in which human agency can be reclaimed through the reassertion of the contingencies of space and time, articulated through the reconstruction of human communities of interaction transcending the individual. Without the contingent understanding of human agency, there can be no space between actions and outcomes and no real agentic choice-making.

In this book, I hope to make a start in undertaking a radical challenge to our human-centred and agent-centred understandings of the world and to suggest that, in articulating problems as a result of human behaviour or decision-making, the problems of the world have become reinterpreted as problems of the human subject itself. In this framework, the solutions are then not seen to lie with structures of economic and social relations but with the social and cognitive shaping of the lives of those who are often seen to be the most marginal and powerless. This shift, from the material problems of the external world to the subjective problems of human thought and action, has been concomitant with the shift from state-based to society-based understandings of the world and the critique of liberal rationalist assumptions of the subject. As a consequence of this shift, we can understand human-centred approaches as reflecting the end of the transformative aspirations of the Enlightenment project: as the exhaustion of the liberal project of modernity. In coming to a close, it appears to show that the removal of the understanding of the human as distinct from the world – as a transformative subject – means that freedom (the sphere of human autonomy) is inevitably problematized. In this problematization it appears that by necessity – in a global and complex world – governance needs to be imposed wherever autonomy appears. It seems therefore clear that human-centred approaches have shrunk rather than enlarged our world and have restricted our understanding of transformative possibilities. Work on the human rather than upon the world we live in is a never-ending process of critique of our creative and transformative capacities and, as a programme of post-liberal governance, can only constitute the end of the political project of enlarging human freedom.

2 | FROM FREEDOM TO NECESSITY

Introduction

This chapter seeks to draw out the consequences of our perception of the end of liberal modernity: the sense that we can no longer learn and develop as part of a goal-oriented process of engagement in the external world. If there is no meaningful process connecting our actions and their final consequences we are no longer able to make adjustments according to a process of human development or human freedom. Every action would in this sense be final and irreparable. In this framework of understanding, the world of necessity – the complex processes, both natural and social, within which we act and react – can never be fully amenable to human knowledge, control and direction. In which case, rather than necessity becoming the precondition for freedom, the critique of our hubristic belief in human freedom is leading us to the appreciation of necessity. It is the end of human freedom, as we have traditionally conceptualized it, once we recognize that our choices need to be shaped by necessity rather than freedom. In the world we live in today, we are held no longer to be free subjects, capable of taming necessity with the goal of human freedom: rather, human freedom is constructed in terms of adapting to necessity.

In the sections which follow, it will be emphasized that human freedom to experiment and to struggle and engage in the world depends on a temporal gap between our actions as human agents and the outcome or ends of struggles or experiments. This gap is mediated by an understanding of structures of meaning into which our actions can be meaningfully inserted. This gap is that of meaningful contingency. What we understand as meaningful contingency is the possibility that we can turn necessity into freedom. It is this gap which enables us to learn from failures of the past and develop our own understanding and knowledge of the world we live in. This learning necessarily involves the appreciation that we can always have a second chance to do things better in our ongoing engagement in the process of shaping our external world. It is precisely this possibility of a second chance, or of improvement or progress, which is denied us in a world we are told is globalized, or in a world composed of complex overlapping processes of action and reaction, and therefore not amenable to direct human understanding and control.

This chapter goes on to explore the human-centred problematic as one in which we no longer have the 'freedom to err'. The removal of human freedom under today's discourses of human-centred governance has not been conceptualized by voices critical of changing forms of governmental rule. One of the key reasons for this is that, as briefly discussed in the previous chapter, for most critical analysts of power, the liberal discourse of the freedom of the subject still plays a crucial role in understanding the forms and limits of government power. This understanding of freedom, so central to liberal discourses demarcating the limits to government, can no longer operate under today's assumptions of the compression of time and space under globalization. In the globalized conception of the world we can have human agency but never fixed structures of meaning separating human agency from the appearance of the world: there is no longer any mediating of human responsibility through the separation of agency and structure.[1] In a world which can only be understood as a problematic product of human agency, the burden of responsibility must necessarily remove human freedom.

The end of freedom

Today, there is a new consensus that human freedom is at best a myth, constructed by the consoling secular beliefs of liberal modernity, and, at worst, a declaration of human hubris and a sign that the human is the biggest danger to the planet which we inhabit. We construct our critique of human freedom through the critique of what we now knowingly dismiss as liberalism: the belief that humans are rational and autonomous beings capable of ruling themselves in their and society's best interests. Everywhere we look, the world appears to confirm the hubris explicit in the idea of human freedom. If we choose to, we can see the consequence of free human choices in man-made global warming and the potential destruction of our planet. It is possible for us to see the hubris of human freedom in the greed of the bankers and free market governments, which created the global financial crisis and then passed on the costs to the rest of society. We can perhaps see the hubris of ideas of human freedom in the poor choice-making of the majority of people in our own societies who refuse to save for retirement, who overeat, parent poorly, smoke and do not exercise enough. In international relations we might see the hubris of ideas of human freedom wherever we cast our gaze: in the catastrophic failure of the 'liberation' of the Iraqi people from the rule of Saddam Hussein; in the failure of the similar, but lower-profile, intervention of 'liberating' the people of Afghanistan; in conflict in sub-Saharan Africa; or perhaps in the slow pace of progress in peace-building and democratic reform in places like Bosnia or Kosovo.

Rather than a belief in human progress we understand the problems of our world as products of the human belief in the teleology of progress: as caused by our naive belief in human freedom. We live in a world that appears to be out of the conscious control of humanity. It seems naive to imagine that humanity can come up with solutions to the problems of our world. We appear to have lost the belief that new technology or scientific advances will benefit the world, rather than merely reproduce or increase problems of inequality and environmental destruction. We now often believe that humans are not so special; that we are not somehow subjects separate from or distinct from the world in which we live (this is captured well in 'post-human' frameworks of understanding; see, for a useful summary, Cudworth and Hobden 2011). Instead, we realize that we are entirely embedded in and dependent upon our external environment and our social contexts. In fact, we suffer precisely from our human illusion that we are free. Our freedom, our subjective capacity for thinking and decision-making, appears as our particularly 'human' curse. The combination of our advances in science and technology and the globalization of our world makes human freedom – human action and decision-making – particularly problematic. As Cudworth and Hobden note, our human properties of consciousness and reflectiveness, coupled with the relational social power that operates both between humans and between humans and the non-human world, have serious consequences for both humans and non-humans alike (ibid.: 49). Rather than being singled out by God as being made in his image, with the capacity for creation and for transforming our environment, we understand our social powers as the biggest threat both to ourselves and to the planet upon which we live.

It could be argued that human freedom – human action and choice-making and their potentially destructive consequences – is not a novel project of concern. At least since the invention of the atomic bomb and its destructive use in Hiroshima and Nagasaki and the catastrophic social and political engineering of Hitler's Germany and Stalin's Russia, we have been aware of the need to limit and constrain human freedom. However, as long as there was a political contestation over the direction of society, a construction of political modernity in the familiar terms of left and right, human freedom – human action and choice-making – could never be seen completely negatively. We understood that whatever human beings had done could be undone, whatever human action had destroyed could be rebuilt, whatever mistakes or errors humans made could be corrected and could be learnt from (see Arendt 2005: 155–7). We understood that the horrors of the nuclear bomb meant that war had to be opposed, and if not opposed at least regulated and limited, as the cause of peace became linked inextricably with those of socialism and justice. We understood that the crimes of Hitler's Germany or Stalin's Russia were not inevitable, but were the results of social and political struggles, defeats of liberal constitutional projects or perhaps of proletarian projects of world revolution.

Under liberal modernity, human freedom was seen as providing the answers and creative possibilities for overcoming the potential disastrousness of the world. We looked back at the past and understood the world within a grand narrative of progress. We understood that the human world was a contingent world where projects of change or of liberation could fail as well as succeed, as much as projects of conservatism or reaction could be resisted, fought and opposed. As long as the world was constructed as a world of politics – a world of left and right – human action and human agency were necessarily assumed to be capable of overcoming problems and transforming the world in which we lived and struggled.

Structures and contingency: Prigogine versus Newton

The ending of liberal modernity can be usefully understood as entry into a world without the possibility of learning from processes of mediation: without a meaningful gap or structure between our actions and their consequences. In the complexity of globalized processes we are increasingly aware that we have no control over what happens after we act. Without fixed and meaningful structures, in which our choices can be understood, there is no way of managing their consequences. In this framing, it is as if our acts or decisions were final or immediate. This sense of a lack of a gap between our actions and their consequences, which we often describe in terms of living in a globalized world, does not necessarily mean that our actions have immediate effects temporaneously. As we are aware, it may take years, in the case of smoking, or generations, in the case of carbon dioxide pollution, for these behavioural choices to have their terrible and catastrophic effects on our health or that of the planet. However, because the processes which are unleashed, or that our actions are inserted into, shift beyond our conscious control, it appears that the consequences are immediate ones. They are immediate, not in the sense that they occur without a temporal gap but because they appear to be undoable: they appear to be final and irrevocable.

Without a temporal gap constituted by the construction of structures external to and independent of our actions, there can be no gap between the human and the world. There can be no contingent relations through which we learn or progress (either as individuals or collectively), and therefore we never have the possibility to act upon our mistakes or to have another chance. This aspect of having a second chance is crucial to our understanding of the interplay of structure and agency. The essence of human freedom is the 'freedom to err', the freedom to make mistakes or to fail.[2] Unless failure can be borne, accepted or tolerated there can be no freedom of decision-making. The 'freedom to err' is not another way of stating that we, as agents, do not bear responsibility for our actions.[3] In fact, its meaning is the opposite. We only have freedom as human agents or actors if we can understand our decisions within meaningful structures or processes. The constitution of ourselves as agents and the constitution of our external world as meaningful can only take place through this process of learning and development at both an individual and a collective and historical level. We can freely take responsibility for our actions only if we are able to learn from them as part of a process of our own development. This means that freedom exists only in the contingent gap between the start of our action and its final conclusion or end. Without this sense of a contingent broader social contribution we would find it impossible to act as agents or subjects or to bear the burden of failure.[4] It is in the space created by this gap that we can construct and pursue our own goals. Without the freedom to err – the freedom to learn and develop – we would not be able to construct or pursue human goals. It is in the process of constructing human goals that we enlarge our freedom, both individually and collectively.

Today's globalized and complex world appears to demonstrate the dominance of necessity over freedom in that the advances in science and technology and human knowledge are not seen as increasing human freedom but as threatening the very existence of the human. It seems that we are on the verge of environmental or financial global crisis precisely because we have failed to learn that we cannot successfully consciously shape or control the complex and interconnected processes within which we act. The immediacy of actions and consequences, in a world understood to be globalized, removes the contingency of the gap between actions and outcomes and, in so doing, removes the possibility of human progress. This shift from a liberal or modernist teleology, which presupposed external or natural laws, independent of human action, and therefore promised the potential for human development, is now often dismissed as a Newtonian fallacy. In today's sensibilities we are much more likely to be drawn towards physicist Ilya Prigogine's view of complexity as 'the irreversible succession of events' where 'the arrow of time' ensures that circumstances are never stable for repeatable cause-and-effect relations, destabilizing any possibility of acting on the basis of knowable eternal or fixed 'natural' laws (Prigogine 2003: 56; see also Stengers 2011: 105–22; Connolly 2004).

Our conceptions of human progress depended upon meaningful contingency, on the existence of external laws or structures, which we could aspire to know and understand and act upon. We could aspire to transform necessity into freedom only when we understood ourselves as acting within meaningful natural or social processes, or structures, which existed outside of and beyond our own individual actions. Prior to our modern age, we were slaves to necessity and could not conceive of universal human freedom.[5] Under conceptions of Enlightenment modernity, freedom became possible through the overcoming or transformation of necessity: turning the external world – of necessity – from an alien and unknowable world into a human world, amenable to human action, human goals and human aspirations. As Engels wrote in *Anti-Dühring*:

> Hegel was the first to state correctly the relation between freedom and necessity. To him, freedom is the insight into necessity (*die*

Einsicht in die Notwendigheit). 'Necessity is *blind* only *in so far as it is not understood* [begriffen].' Freedom does not consist in any dreamt-of independence from natural laws, but in the knowledge of these laws, and in the possibility this gives of systematically making them work towards definite ends. This holds good in relation both to the laws of external nature and to those which govern the bodily and mental existence of men themselves ... (Engels 1947: Part 1, ch. XI, p. 6)

The space between our actions and their outcomes is that of contingency. We are able to cope with contingency in a world understood as amenable to human progress. In which case, everything that happens or occurs in the world, no matter how dreadful, provides us with a new basis for knowledge and understanding.

As Engels stated, freedom was not understood as existing in opposition to necessity. Freedom did not exist in a flight from necessity – in a withdrawal from the world, which seems alien or threatening. Freedom existed only in a contestation or challenge to necessity – in overcoming or transforming what was alien to us into human knowledge which then could be applied in the enhancement of human progress. Necessity was understood to subject us precisely because we did not understand it and therefore we had no human freedom – no humanly chosen ends – in relation to it. The expansion of human ends – of free human choice-making – was conceived as the history of human culture and of the separation of the human from the world of natural necessity. For Engels, this transformation, from necessity to freedom, could be historically drawn teleologically – from the invention of fire by friction, which 'gave man for the first time control over one of the forces of nature', to the invention of the steam engine, which drove the Industrial Revolution, and beyond (ibid.: 7).

Freedom, in fact, involved the appreciation of necessity. Even radical thinkers, such as Lenin, argued that mankind 'must necessarily and inevitably adapt themselves to the necessity of natural laws' (Lenin 1972: III, ch. 6, p. 2). In fact, he went as far as to argue that we can talk of 'blind necessity' of the operation of the external world unknown to us: of 'unknown necessity' (ibid.). The difference between this understanding of the world and that of today's dominant framings is in the way in which freedom was understood in relation to necessity. For radical thought, human freedom depended upon a dynamic understanding of the relationship between freedom and necessity. The external world thereby constituted an ongoing and unlimited realm of possibilities for human freedom precisely because this world was understood to be structured through meaningful contingency: 'the recognition of the objective reality of the external world and of the laws of external nature, and of the fact that this world and these laws are fully knowable to man but can never be known to him with finality' (ibid.: 3).[6]

The social construction of structures

The active appreciation of necessity as a problematic through which freedom can be exercised and expanded depends upon our broader conception of ourselves as acting subjects in the world. It is human action and human development which turn 'blind necessity' into forces amenable to human use and understanding and thereby turn necessity into freedom. To begin to construct structures of meaning, which enable us to aspire to freedom through the taming or transformation of necessity, requires that we have a sense of engagement in a collective process or project, whether that is understood in narrow professional terms or broader political terms, regardless of how these are specifically constructed. It is these collective relationships and their meaningful construction within broader discourses or grand narratives which enabled us to understand necessity as the driving process of human development or human freedom – as 'the mother of invention', according to some versions of Plato's *The Republic* (Plato n.d.: Book II).

Probably the theorist with the richest appreciation of the need to understand freedom within the social construction of meaningful structures of mediation, i.e. of scientific, social, political, religious or natural laws, was Hannah Arendt. She echoed Engels, Lenin and other critical theorists in the appreciation that the world extends only insofar as necessity is open to us to facilitate our understanding and development; whereas the world which cannot be comprehended meaningfully by us – the world of 'blind necessity' – constitutes the end of our world, precisely because it is not amenable to our appropriation as a meaningful structure within which we can consciously engage (and, in the process, expand our meaningful world). As she stated: 'All laws first create a space in which they are valid, and this space is the world in which we can move about in freedom. What lies outside this space is without law, and even more precisely, without world; as far as human community is concerned, it is a desert' (Arendt 2005: 190).

Today, in Arendtian terms, 'the desert' is understood to be expanding as we place much more importance on the limits to our knowledge and understanding.[7] In articulating our world in this way, we acknowledge that we have hubristically exaggerated the realm of freedom while underestimating the realm of blind necessity. It is clear that this historic shift in our appreciation of the relationship between freedom and necessity, like all social knowledge, is a product of political and ideological contestation. The problematic of necessity and freedom today cannot be grasped in the purely objective terms considered of prime importance to radical and critical theorists of the late nineteenth and early twentieth centuries. This problematic is not one which can be technically solved through the extension of scientific knowledge. As Gillott and Kumar point out, our lack of belief in science as making human progress possible appears to have less to do with the discovery of scientific limits to knowledge than with our broader social sensibilities (Gillott and Kumar 1995). Technically or objectively, humanity is consistently making gains in scientific knowledge and in the transformation of 'blind necessity' into 'necessity-for-us' – in overcoming the Kantian divide between subject and world, through transforming the unknown 'thing-in-itself' into the known 'thing-for-us' (Lenin 1972: III, ch. 6, p. 3). Nothing has changed objectively speaking, in that despite scientific advance and the extension of human freedom we, as humans, are still subordinate to necessity insofar as we lack knowledge and therefore influence over many areas of the external world.

What has changed drastically is our subjective understanding of ourselves in relation to the world and the importance that we attach to our subordination to necessity rather than to the sphere of human freedom. Our appreciation of human freedom is a subjective product of political and social contestation and also a product of our political and social experiences and expectations. It is dependent on the strength of our collectively and socially constructed understandings of ourselves within structures of spatial and temporal communities of engagement with our external world. The construction of ourselves as agents, collectively engaged in achieving external transformation, is the precondition for us to act as agents in a world of meaningful structures: in a world of laws.

This set of shared assumptions was vital in enabling us to act as subjects, to understand that we do not alone bear the burdens and responsibilities of our actions: that beyond our individual acts lies a greater force capable of making up for our own personal limitations and finitude. On the basis of an arbitrary – or finite – individual life, necessity always appears to dominate over freedom, whereas in the longer time-span of human history it is easier to see freedom increasing as the realm of ignorance or of 'blind necessity' diminishes.[8] At the heart of the relationship between human freedom and necessity is not only the objective understanding of human progress – in terms of culture, knowledge, technology and economic, social and political modernity – but also, and fundamentally, the social sense of connection between ourselves as individuals and our wider society. The less sense of social connection we have, the less we are immersed in structures or frameworks of collective meaning and the more we confront the world as finite and vulnerable individuals.

The less collective mediation between ourselves and the world, the more we appear to be ruled by necessity rather than by freedom. This is because freedom is meaningless at the level of the individual – to rule ourselves as individuals would be to submit ourselves entirely to the rule of blind or arbitrary necessity. Freedom, in terms of our ability to construct ourselves as meaningful actors in a meaningful world, depends on the spatial and temporal structures of both action and decision-making. These are both temporal and spatial, in terms of the need for meaningful human collectivities and for structures of regularity in the external world, which enable us to make sense of the past and to project our actions into a meaningful future through which contingency can be managed. Law as a spatial and temporal construction gives meaning – gives structure – to our contingent human world.

In the world structured by the development of meaningful contingency, humanity was able to generate an understanding of the meaningfulness of our actions as future-oriented, despite the contingent gap between actions and outcomes. We did this through the collective narratives produced through the strength of our social connections, with friends, family, colleagues, comrades and others. It is only through an understanding of our individual lives as part of meaningful collective structures, which are independent of us, which pre-exist and outlive us, that we can understand necessity as generative of freedom. It was these external social and ideological structures of meaning – whether scientific, political or religious – which enabled us to understand our actions as mediated: as part of processes amenable to human understanding and control. These social connections can be understood as constituting the structures of meaningful contingency. Our understanding of the world as structured through meaning, constituted through our social engagement and connection, formed a barrier between our actions and their outcomes: they placed our actions in a broader context both spatially and temporally. It was precisely because of this socially constructed cushion of contingency that the world appeared to be meaningful to us and we could make sense of and learn from human history. Today, in a world of complex processes in which it appears that necessity can no longer be meaningfully understood, we perceive the world to be no longer structured through meaningful contingency.

From freedom to necessity

It is very important to stress that freedom stems from the meaningful contingency of the world. In a global or a globalized world, we are continually confronted with external necessity – with a world of appearances requiring responsive choices but without the possibility of future-oriented human action and understanding. We are always told that we should expect the unexpected and usually the catastrophic. This is well illustrated by the butterfly trope (referred to in the previous chapter): no one would expect the butterfly to flap its wings and cause a hurricane; however, our understanding of the world as comprised of complex processes, held to be overlapping and self-generating, means that we can imagine *causation* without the possibility of prediction or intention ('emergent causality' in the terminology of William Connolly, 2004). However, the processes of causation are so complex and interdependent they appear to be entirely out of our control; understanding, if it is possible at all, is possible only after the event. This is captured well by complexity theory, which suggests that we can model complex interactions but cannot explain the outcomes of these interacting non-linear processes (for example, Cilliers 1998; Kauffman 1995). Meaningfulness, the possibility of us having choice or freedom of action, seems to end as soon as we act on a particular choice or decision. Globalization therefore mediates the gap between our actions and their perceived outcomes through the assertion that we cannot fully predict or understand the complex and fluid processes in which these actions take place (Urry 2003). Our learning takes place only at the level of a response to a final outcome that is observable in the world. Our learning can happen only after the consequences become, in this sense, final, or non-undoable (such as the hurricane in another part of the world). Therefore, in many cases our possibility to experimentally and experientially learn from our actions and decisions no longer exists.

Because there is no meaningful or fixed structure inserted in between our actions and their final outcomes it appears that our actions directly caused the outcomes in the world. The world of appearances is no longer meaningfully mediated and separated from the actions and decisions of human actors. Once meaningful mediation disappears, it appears that human agency *directly* creates the world. Under globalization, human agents therefore are understood as acting and choice-making but without freedom. We cannot control or understand the processes which our actions are seen to create and to be part of, any more than the butterfly can have any further impact on the complexities of the weather. As human subjects we can no longer understand ourselves as consciously acting in the world. Rather than human freedom expanding, with the possibility of new ends or goals, dependent on the increase in our knowledge and capacities to direct and shape our external world, it appears that the external world of necessity is continually expanding and that we need to transform ourselves as actors and decision-makers in order to adapt to the external world.

Human freedom necessarily implies the possibility of controlling and directing change, of learning and experimenting as part of an ongoing process.[9] We are free when we decide on a project in the world, can take responsibility for it and act and react in relation to the goals we aim for and learn from the setbacks. However, under globalization, the processes we set in train appear to leave our control as soon as we act on a decision. They only come back to bite us from behind as final consequences which it is too late to change. We lack freedom precisely because actions cannot be related to goals without the meaningful mediation of structures. Our action appears to have consequences directly, immediately – i.e. without mediation.

A good example is parenting. Not so long ago we believed that parenting was a highly mediated act: that how we parented was a process of learning and individual decision-making with a wide range of freedom in parenting styles, as we believed that how we parented probably made little difference to final outcomes, which were richly mediated through social class, economic environment, chance and other factors. Today, we are much more likely to believe that how we parent has a direct causal impact on the final outcomes in terms of our children's future health and happiness. We believe this so strongly that we think that one wrong action or one wrong choice, in how children are treated or disciplined, can have irreparable consequences. What is worse is that these irreparable consequences may not be immediately visible or ascertainable. Our inability to understand and control the complex processes at work means that we are continually working backwards from problematic appearances in the world – for example, a child's problems at school – to causes which we bear responsibility for. At the same time, we often appear paralysed in terms of imagining how we might already have caused future problems or difficulties.

Another example is that of smoking, exercising and other personal health choices. In the past, we believed that barring chance or genetic misfortune we all lived for approximately the same lifespan, depending on general levels of eco-social development. Now we tend to believe that we are directly responsible for our own health and lifespan (this is analysed in greater detail in the following chapter on resilience). It is important to note that it is not the case that we feel increasingly responsible for our health because the public provision of healthcare may be or has been cut back. Rather, we understand that health can be directly affected by a wide range of specific choices, in relation to exercise, eating meat, salt intake, exposure to the sun, etc. We believe that it is easy for us to make poor choices, which can irreparably damage our health despite the fact that these were seen as issues of minor importance at the time. Precisely because we could not understand, predict or control the complex processes at work linking actions to outcomes, potentially many years later, we work backwards from health outcomes to causes which we (or someone else) appear to be responsible for.

If we imagined that we could never possibly know in advance, or at the time of our actions or decisions, however minor, what their ultimate ends or outcomes would be, we would become incapacitated, rather than freed, by our choice-making capacities. We could not make free choices because we lacked the meaningful structures through which we could aspire to create our own ends. In a globalized world, we no longer have the sense of a capacity to choose our own ends – a sense of freedom. Instead we have merely a world of necessity, which appears to dictate to us how we should act in order to respond and adapt to our external environment. Choice-making then becomes merely a question of necessity – of responsibility – not of freedom. If we increasingly imagine that the world is created by us and by our decisions and actions, we feel, both individually and collectively, increasingly responsible for the world. This shift can be seen particularly in the face of disasters and catastrophes, which we previously might have understood to be accidents of 'fate' or of 'nature'. Now these disasters are often understood as warnings about man-made global warming or of too much consumption; in the same way, many people felt responsible, or ascribed responsibility to others, for the actions of the 9/11 terrorists – again, as if these were brought about, or *caused*, by Western consumer society or Western foreign policy (see Baudrillard's acute observations, 2002).

The key point that needs to be stressed about this inversion of a liberal teleology is that *causation* entirely replaces *intention* as a framework of critique and understanding. Meaning and responsibility are traced back to the behaviours of individuals and societies as a framework for making judgements and for arguing for societal changes, but intentionality is entirely lacking. Intentionality implies forward-looking agency. In this framework of working backwards to understand the cause of problems, or appearances or events in the world, intention is removed. With the removal of intentionality as a guide to good or bad behavioural choices we move towards the regulation of society – good governance – that operates outside or beyond a liberal discourse based on the choice-making freedoms of the rational subject. This shift or inversion in liberal understandings of the relationship between the subject and the world then becomes the starting point for the frameworks of post-liberal governance regulation and institutional understandings which work back from appearance to behavioural choices and then farther back to the cognitive contexts in which those choices are made.

In a historic reversal of liberal frameworks of government, and liberal teleologies of progress, there is no longer the telos of transforming necessity into freedom. Under liberal modernity, the development of the productive forces of society and of science and technology were held to liberate mankind, freeing the human from the ties and constraints of nature and the drudgery of labour. In this world, choice-making was understood to increase as a sphere of human freedom (Marx and Engels 1970: 54). Today, the opposite is the case: choice-making is held to increase as a sign of unfreedom or of necessity. In our agent-centred world, the increased importance of choice-making may be an outcome of the increase in science and technology but this is no longer necessarily equated with a teleology of human progress. Choice-making is held to increase in importance precisely because the problems of our external environment – whether those of poverty, conflict, inequality or environmental degradation – are seen to stem directly from human activity and human choice-making. We have to increasingly act to reshape choices out of the necessity imposed upon us through the understanding of the human shaping of the world. We therefore focus on choice, not as a sign of freedom but because we increasingly recognize the idea of freedom to be illusory. In this way, choice-making symbolizes the problems of human nature, manifested in the problematic effects of our choice-making actions. This problematic of choice-making, imposed on us by the world we live in, is not a liberation or a process of freedom, but is seen as a dangerous process, ever threatening our own destruction – and as a human problem to which there can be no conclusive solution.

The mechanism through which human freedom was understood to operate is precisely that which is seen to enslave us. The fact that we make choices and make the world, although we are understood to be ill equipped to foresee or appreciate the effects or consequences of these actions, makes the human subject a dangerous and problematic one and constitutes human freedom as a grave threat to the world. This transformation of choice-making from being constitutive of freedom to being constitutive of rule through necessity cannot properly be grasped without an understanding of this shifting context and of the assumptions upon which post-liberalism operates.

Although it may seem counter-intuitive, our understanding of globalization highlights the social and cultural consensus which accepts the removal of the contingency of human action and decision-making. In a globalized world we understand that there is much less mediation between our actions and their consequences. As time and space become compressed we are increasingly aware that everything we do has consequences. How we parent, how we consume, what we consume, how we act, can seem much more important. The less we understand our actions and decisions within frameworks of grand narratives, traditions and collective experiences, the more immediately we seem to confront the world. The more immediately and the less mediation with which we confront the world, the more responsible we appear for our decisions and our actions and the more difficult it is to share the burden of responsibility for failures or mistakes and to act confidently as agents in the world. Our freedom therefore appears to us personally, as individuals, as a burden rather than as an opportunity for creation or transformation.

Nietzsche was probably the first theorist to recognize the importance of the mediation between man and the world. In his aphorism on 'The fable of intelligible freedom' he was keen to critique the error of 'moral responsibility', which confuses human action with outcomes in the world: the error in which 'we take the effect to be the cause' and thereby understand the world as the product of human nature:

> So we make man responsible in turn for the effects of his actions, then for his actions, then for his motives and finally for his nature. Ultimately we discover that his nature cannot be responsible either, in that it is itself an inevitable consequence, an outgrowth of the elements and influences of past and present things; that is man cannot be made responsible for anything, neither for his nature, nor his motives, nor his actions, nor the effects of his actions.
> (1984: 43)

Once we understand that man is directly responsible for the effects humanity has in the world – once the effects of human action become immediately understood as causes – humanity loses the contingency between action and outcome. Nietzsche argued that without this contingency, which is denied in ascriptions of moral responsibility for the world, man is denied genuine responsibility for his actions and is denied any 'freedom of the will' (ibid.: 43). If we lived in a world with no meaningful gap between actions and outcomes there would be no space for development, and we could not be properly moral or free beings. We would bear responsibility for the world, not as free-willed, choice-bearing actors, but as problematic subjects who are unable to free ourselves from limited or irrational choice-making.

The world as it appears would be evidence that human freedom was both illusory and dangerous.

In emphasizing the importance of the end of liberal conceptions of the freedom of the subject, for every aspect of our understanding of politics and policy-making, I therefore choose to use the concept of post-liberal rather than concepts which stress the essential continuities with liberalism, such as 'neoliberalism', 'late liberalism' or 'advanced liberalism'. Post-liberal understandings of governance do not operate around a sphere of liberal limits constituted by the freedom of the subject. Under post-liberalism, freedom is transformed or transmuted into necessity. Freedom becomes transformed into necessity because without the mediation of meaningful structures, separating our actions from the world of appearances, we are all immediately responsible for the world of effects, for the world as it is.

Contingency and politics

The end of grand narratives or meta-narratives, constructing and giving meaning to contingency, has not freed us but rather has ended our ability to conceive of human freedom. The difficulty of constructing the human subject as separate from the world of appearances is reflected in the shrinking of the possibilities of and the space of politics. Politics cannot exist without the possibility of contingency, without the space between actions and outcomes. All political projects necessarily operate in the space of contingency and, in fact, are constitutive of contingent understandings of the world. Politics is externally oriented and future oriented; as an activity it involves people coming together collectively to engage in changing or altering the circumstances under which they live. Any project subordinating individuals to a collectivity and engaging in the task of transforming the external world involves the contingency of meaningful structures both spatially and temporally. Spatially, the forming of a collectivity involves the articulation of shared meanings to which individuals can be bound, such as a party programme or another set of beliefs. Temporally, a political project involves the shared understanding of the world as a set of structures open to understanding and transformation. Human freedom is presupposed in the assumption of free choice in articulating shared beliefs and understandings and in standing apart from the world to engage in a project of change or transformation, the outcomes of which can only ever be understood as contingent.

Without contingency, political engagement or political struggle could not be meaningfully understood.

The grand narratives of left and right, with us since the birth of liberal modernity with the French Revolution, no longer appear to have the capacity to construct a meaningful mediation between human actions and effects in the world: i.e. to structure meaningful political projects. Just as it is impossible to act in the world as an individual subject without a temporal and spatial understanding of the necessary contingency of our actions, so is it impossible to act as a collective representative of society or of social agency. While we still have the legacies of liberal modernity – in representative government, political parties, elections, etc. – it is difficult for representative models to operate without shared frameworks of collective political meaning. It is difficult for governments to take responsibility for policy outcomes without strong mediating frameworks of political participation and social engagement, given meaning and legitimacy by political ideologies or programmes of social change. Liberal modernity was shaped by the understanding of government as capable of wielding social power as part of a political tradition or national narrative shared with the public. This narrative enabled liberal forms of government to evolve through standing over and above social contestation, demarcating clear divisions and limits between the state and society.

Today, government appears to be a burden rather than an opportunity. Those with the 'freedoms' of power feel the responsibility of power but do not have a framework in which their actions and decisions can be understood in a greater historical or political context of ideological contestation. From the position of government, political power seems to have evaporated, along with the frameworks of meaning of left and right. Rather than representing a public power – dependent upon the construction of a meaningful collective – government seems reduced to a private power, looked down upon as a source of patronage, dirty dealing and corruption. In this context, public power genuinely does disappear or appears as unjust, arbitrary or irrational. Governments are therefore at the cutting edge of the attack on human freedom. This should not be understood in the old-fashioned forms of totalitarianism or state censorship and police regulation, or as organized against social or political threats to stability. The attack on human freedom takes the form of the argument that governments do not have the freedoms of decision-making power which they had, or assumed that they had, in the past. Today, governments are always asserting that they are forced to act out of necessity, never out of free choice. The programme of government is always presented as a necessary response to the problems of the world as it appears. Political competition between political parties is rarely posed in terms of freely chosen aims or aspirations, but rather on the basis of their technical or administrative efficiency in governing through necessity.

The key point, with regard to the problematization of freedom, is that governance as the rule of necessity has effects beyond merely hollowing out the public sphere. These effects concern the relationship of government to society, and particularly with regard to the traditional liberal understanding of the barriers between the public and private spheres: the ways in which the freedom of the subject was understood to both constitute liberal power and to limit it. While governments argue that their policy-making is a matter of technical or administrative necessity, they also assert that the limit to their administration of necessity is the area of choice-making freedom of their citizens and those of other states or societies. While governments assert that they have embraced necessity and the problems of the global world and have learnt to rule through necessity, they also assert that their citizens have been much slower in adapting to the rapid changes and challenges of globalization. We have all heard the governmental refrain of the gap between citizens and those who govern: that it is the citizenry who are resistant to change or have unrealistic or outdated expectations about what government can do or achieve. Once government has learnt to rule through necessity rather than freedom, the problems of society can only appear to be those caused through the 'free' choices of the citizenry.

The problematic of freedom is thereby transferred from the sphere of government, from the public sphere, to the sphere of society, to the private sphere. The agent-centred or human-centred understanding, focusing on the capacities and choices of the individual in society, makes freedom the basis of necessity through the removal of the traditional liberal division of the public and the private. The private sphere of inequality and difference is elevated as the only remaining sphere which still operates on the basis of freedom and of autonomous choice-making. In transferring freedom of choice-making to the private sphere, this sphere is problematized as a barrier to the recognition that necessity should be the guide to choice-making. The understanding that the world as it appears is a product of human hubris requiring the limitation of freedom and the acceptance of necessity is no longer an understanding limited to the formal political sphere – as it was in the time when the main threat to the world was understood to be nuclear weapons under the control of states (see, further, Arendt 2005: 190). In the post-liberal world, the critique of human freedom no longer merely threatens to lead to the death of politics as a public activity, leaving the stunted legacy of human freedom in the positive understanding of the individual freedoms of the private sphere (ibid.).

Today's state-endorsed critique of human freedom focuses not on the public sphere of state policy-making but on the private sphere of society – it is here that we are told that people think they can smoke and not exercise and expect to live for ever, or think they can have families but not take responsibility for their moral upbringing, or consume and throw away waste with no concern for the environment, or borrow money and not expect to go into debt. For post-liberal governance, the private sphere – not the public sphere – becomes the area in which it is necessary to encourage and develop active citizenship. The task of the active citizen is to embrace necessity rather than freedom, through realizing the consequences of private individual choice-making. The construction of private choice-making as the cause of societal problems, from crime to unemployment and environmental degradation, removes the final vestiges of liberal conceptions of freedom as a positive attribute or aspiration.

Without a positive understanding of human freedom as the capacity for free choice-making, including the capacity to err, the contingency of human action entirely disappears from the world. The world then becomes the self-product of the individuals composing society without any social mediation of contingency. Once freedom is understood only negatively, the concept of human freedom disappears as a meaningful goal. As we shall see in the following chapters, in human-centred discourses the problematic of human choice-making and actions and the difficulties of accepting the responsibilities of rule by necessity are conceived of as barriers to 'freedom'. We are 'unfree' precisely because liberal modernity convinced us that freedom lay in the pursuit of self-determined goals rather than in understanding the necessary limits imposed by our responsibilities to others and to our environment. Once we free ourselves of these illusions then we are 'free' to become responsible citizens, acting in tune with our social relations and responsive to the needs of others. Freedom is, in this sense, akin to a process of self-realization or self-transformation, rather than intimately bound up with our goal-directed transformation of our external world. It is little wonder then that radical critics of modern liberal conceptions of politics argue that we need to turn to non-Western ways of understanding, such as those offered by Mahatma Gandhi or Confucius. As radical democratic theorist Fred Dallmayr argues: 'human freedom from this angle is limited or circumscribed not by the state or external procedures but by the ability of ethical transformation, that is, the ability of people to rule themselves rather than ruling others' (2010: 180).

We think that we are free as decision-making individuals only if we lack the ability to properly understand the need to welcome the rule of necessity, through becoming 'other-regarding'; enabling the external world of people, non-humans and our environment to guide our behavioural choices. As long as we do not freely welcome the rule of necessity, our freedom is a trap that can only be, at best, illusory and, at worst, dangerous. The privileging of necessity over freedom can take place only through a thoroughgoing critique of the misplaced and hubristic aspirations of the subject of liberal modernity. This subject is increasingly characterized as needing to be brought back to – to be constrained by or to be embedded in – the world of necessity. Rather than understanding human freedom as the product of 'the enlargement of power or managerial control' over the external world, we are increasingly told that, in fact, 'democratic self-rule has to involve a practice of self-restraint and self-transformation (even self-emptying)' (ibid.: 184; this 'self-emptying' of the subject is precisely the ethical or political aspiration of post-human or new materialist approaches, which emphasize that politics as 'control' needs to be replaced by a political ecology of 'care', Bennett 2010a). This desire to remedy the problems of the world through the transformation of 'the self' – the transforming of the human subject – is one which appears to unite many critical social theorists, working across a diverse range of policy spheres. While self-transformation may sound like a radical goal, it is important to note that this transformation is internally rather than externally oriented. Working on the transformation of self, while reifying the external world, extends the realm of necessity rather than the realm of freedom.

Conclusion

In today's terminology of human-centred approaches, the end of freedom and the embrace of necessity are expressed most clearly in terms of the necessity of inculcating resilience. As will be considered in more detail in the following chapter, resilience is the key problematic through which the freedom of decision-making is re-posed in terms of necessity. Resilient subjects are held to be able to respond to external circumstances in ways that enable them to make choices with effective, efficient and non-problematic outcomes. Resilience is the goal of agent-centred policy-making, which no longer assumes the state-based programmatic framework of the goals and practices of liberal government. Resilience is not amenable to liberal frameworks of understanding: working on individuals neither as the bearers of liberal rights and freedoms nor as rational interest-bearing subjects. The subjects of resilience are subjects constructed through necessity, not through their free choice. The human-centred discourse of resilience directly links the appearance of the world to the actions of individuals and thereby necessarily sees the most poor, marginal and conflict-ridden as in most need of resilience. The resilient subject is not constituted as a subject through its self-activity but rather its self-activity enables it to be constituted as an object of rule.

3 | RESILIENCE: THE SELF-PRODUCTION OF SOCIETY

Introduction

Under human-centred regimes of understanding, societies are no longer conceived of as collectivities capable of being secured or developed by governments. Instead of states managing, directing, shaping or controlling social processes, societies are increasingly understood as complex self-producing processes or systems. Rather than societies' processes being understood as inserted into broader social and economic relations, we tend towards institutionalist understandings of societal differences or agent- or actor-oriented theories, which suggest that societies can increasingly be understood, upon their own terms, as self-constituting.[1] In this case, the state can no longer stand above or separate to society but equally cannot leave society's self-production to itself. One of the clearest examples of this shifting understanding of the role of the state in the problematic of social self-production is that of the discourse of resilience and societal security. In this framework of considering a wide range of societal questions, the assumption is that state intervention is needed on the basis that the problems of the self-constituted world can be addressed only at source, at the level of the individuals and communities which compose society.

Resilience is defined here as positive adaptation or the active embrace of necessity; the resilient subject is one which actively embraces necessity through positive adaptation. The resilient subject (at both individual and collective levels) is not passive in the face of necessity and does not seek to resist external changes in circumstances, but rather is active, understanding necessity as the only facilitator of self-knowledge, self-growth and self-transformation. I will argue that resilience is a normative concept, or an ideal type. There is no such thing as a fully resilient subject: resilience is the product of a process which is ongoing and has no end as such. Resilience has to be continually produced and can be measured or calculated only as a comparative or relative quality.[2] Some individuals or communities may be understood to embrace necessity more than others, but none can be understood to be fully resilient, fully open to or embracing of external necessity and cognizant of the consequences of their actions. While we are aware that our fixed understandings derived from the past are a barrier to resilience we are also aware that our thought processes and cultural and social values continue to bound or limit our awareness of necessity. We can only ever be somewhere along the continuum of resilience, and therefore ultimately all are in need of enabling to become more resilient.

In discourses of resilience there is a clear assumption that governments need to assume a more proactive engagement with society. This proactive engagement is understood to be preventive, not in the sense of preventing future disaster or catastrophe but of preventing the disruptive or destabilizing effects of such an event. In this sense, the key to security programmes of resilience is the ability of citizens to respond to security crises. The subject of security thereby shifts from the state to society and to the individuals constitutive of it. In many ways, this shift away from a sovereign-based understanding to a societal understanding of security, under the guidance or goal of resilience, could be understood as a deliberalizing discourse, one which divests security responsibilities from the level of the state down to the level of the citizen. This chapter seeks to consider some of the genealogical aspects of discourses of resilience as a societal or individualized understanding of security (particularly focusing on the work of Friedrich von Hayek and Anthony Giddens) in order to work through some of the consequences of the state's divestment of security responsibilities for classical liberal framings of freedom and autonomy. It thereby seeks to draw out further the ways in which necessity is understood to shape governance interventions in the societal sphere and to impose upon the sphere of private choice-making and behaviour.

Societal resilience

This chapter seeks to further develop some of the themes touched upon in work highlighting the links between discourses of resilience and the shift from a state-based to a society-based understanding of security practices (Edwards 2009; Briggs 2010; Bulley 2011). It seeks to highlight the centrality of the agency of individuals as 'active citizens' in the human-centred discourses of resilience, whereby governance policies and practices shift the focus of security on to the capacities for reasoned responses of the citizenry. Fillipa Lentzos and Nikolas Rose, for example, highlight, in their critique of understandings that security discourses seem to be leading to the securitization of life, that we are witnessing 'perhaps the opposite of a "Big Brother State"' (Lentzos and Rose 2009: 243). Discourses of resilience do not centrally focus upon material attributes (military equipment, technology, welfare provisions, etc.) that can be provided through government as a way of protecting populations or responding after an event. Resilience concerns attributes that cannot be provided by state authorities. For this reason, discourses of resilience do not fit well with traditional liberal framings of security practices as preparatory or preventive or as reactive post-hoc interventions.

As James Brassett and Nick Vaughan-Williams note in their study of UK civil contingencies and trauma resilience training (2011), the focus of resilience practices is less upon the specific 'event' (which can be prepared for or reacted to) and more the internal qualities or capacities for responsive agency at the level of the individual subject. Here, the discussion of trauma is particularly useful as the resilience discourse encourages a shift from post-hoc programmes of trauma counselling to the inculcation of mental or subjective capacities to respond to crises without becoming traumatized (see also O'Malley 2010; Furedi 2007). In this context, the problematic of the inculcation of societal resilience, of the subjective capabilities and capacities needed to respond and adapt to crises, has become a growing focus of governmental concern (see, for example, Walker and Cooper 2011; Coaffee et al. 2009; UK Cabinet Office 2011a).

It appears that resilience practices are transforming security discourses from concerns with external threats to fears over the coping or adaptive capacities of individuals and their communities.[3] Coping capacities are inner qualities possessed by individuals, which are held to enable them to autonomously anticipate and respond to complex circumstances. This shift from a focus on the activity and provision of government to the capacity of citizens to effectively respond to crises – and increasingly to take responsibility for 'self-government' – is of vital importance to our understanding of resilience as a set of discursive practices of governing through agent-centred frameworks of understanding (see, for example, Foucault 2010: 25–40; 2008; O'Malley 2004; Miller and Rose 2008; Rose 1999; Dean 2010). This chapter seeks to draw out further this link between human-centred approaches, focusing on the agency of individuals, and the security discourse of resilience (see, further, for example, Dillon and Reid 2009; Chandler 2010a). Following on from the work of Pat O'Malley, it suggests that the problematic of resilience and the discourses of societal security are: 'not specific to the governance of particular threats, or indeed even to threats per se. It is a technology that is imagined to equip the subject to deal with uncertainty in general' (O'Malley 2010: 505).

The resilience problematic of how society proactively engages with and adapts to uncertainty has been at the heart of recent UK policy discussions on how to empower citizens to be more capable of governing themselves through making better life choices in the face of risk and complexity. This broader discussion locates the threat to societal security not in any specific externally generated 'event' or 'threat' but in the capacity or capability of citizens to proactively take responsibility both for their own security and for those around them (Dean 2011). The discussion of how society could become more self-governing and how government practices could inculcate resilience has been highlighted by the 2008 publication of *Nudge* by Richard Thaler and Cass Sunstein and the recent policy attention given to the importance of individual choice-making by the UK Cabinet Office, UK Prime Minister David Cameron's Behavioural Insight Team (the 'nudge unit') and the Royal Society of Arts' (RSA's) Social Brain project. For these authors and policy groups, the problems of societal security can be both analysed and addressed through capability-building at the level of the decision-making individual.

The starting point for *Nudge* is that people lack the capacity to adapt efficiently to their circumstances and to choose what is best for them; that the modern liberal conception of 'economic man' (*Homo œconomicus*) may work well in economic textbooks but that in the real world real human beings are not very good at making the right choices. It is suggested here that one useful starting point for an understanding of resilience as a discourse of societal security can be found in the distinction made by Thaler and Sunstein between economic man and real human beings – as they state, between 'Econs' and 'Humans'. While economic man can be assumed to always make the right or rational choice, the human often fails, and this failure can have destructive consequences at both the individual and the societal levels. The UK Cabinet Office has taken up these concerns to suggest that governance should focus on how the 'choice environment' is shaped as citizens appear to lack the rational capacities to make the right choices themselves without external 'nudging', 'steering' and 'priming' (IfG 2010). While it could be argued that the UK Cameron/ Clegg government's Behavioural Insight Team or 'nudge unit' has had limited effects on government policy-making (Curtis 2011; Day 2011), there is little doubt that the problematization of citizens as rational choice-making actors has been placed at the centre of the discourse of resilience and security, positing the task of government in terms of governance: improving the choice-making capacity of its citizens.

The work of *Nudge* has helped to cohere the understanding of the subject as lacking in rational capacities to deal with the unexpected events and complexities of our insecure world. Relying heavily on this schema, Charlie Edwards's Demos publication *Resilient Nation* (2009) argues that:

> Thinking about choice architecture is an incredibly useful way of framing how central and local government, emergency planning officers and the emergency services can influence an individual or community's behaviour, especially on issues like risk ... a funda-mentally important task in making society more resilient. Nudges also help ... [by] shifting some of the responsibility of resilience planning and management to communities and individuals ...
> (Ibid.: 42–5)

In the UK, Thaler and Sunstein have been challenged, not for their degraded understanding of individual capacities for choice-making but rather for their underestimation of the problem of choice-shaping (Day 2011; Chakrabortty 2010). The UK Royal Society of Arts' Social Brain project suggests that the problem of societal security is too large for the government to solve on its own, through 'nudging' citizens to make better choices (Grist 2009: 9). Interestingly, the Social Brain project takes up many of the central conceptions outlined in Anthony Giddens's work on *Beyond Left and Right* (1994) and in *The Third Way* (1998) to argue that governance requires a reorientation around the politics of individual choice to construct citizens who are able to respond to the problems of risk autonomously and responsibly:

> ... life politics is the politics of choice in a deep existential sense
> – a politics where one is aware of what it is like to live reflexively

in a post-traditional and globalised world … Whether we like it or not, in late modernity citizens need to be able to reflexively chart their way through the choppy waters of a globalised economy. And whether we like it or not, they need to find ways of changing the way they live if they are to counteract problems like entrenched inequality and environmental degradation … The kind of person enabled by politics to face up to the challenges of late modernity Giddens calls an 'autotelic' self … an autotelic self is really just an autonomous and responsible citizen. (Grist 2009: 16)

The RSA propose an active programme of governance on the basis of the need to empower modern citizens as individuated decision-makers in order to inculcate resilience through overcoming their lack of rational decision-making capacities:

wholly rational individuals do not need the support of publicly-engaged institutions and associative groups to aid their decision-making about the issues of life politics. They simply need to be fed information and, given their rationality, correct responses will inexorably follow. Yet people are not isolated and wholly self-interested … And neither are they wholly rational – left to their individual devices they may make bad decisions that economists would consider 'irrational'. (Ibid.: 29)

The project of governing for social resilience is asserted to depend upon 'the limits of personal choice' and the development of knowledge of 'how autonomy and responsibility are produced' (ibid.). For the Social Brain project, the key to this new knowledge is that of 'neurological reflexivity': a greater understanding of the working and limits of the human brain (ibid.: 33). Through a greater use of emotional and cognitive self-awareness, the RSA suggests that 'people might gain more power over themselves by using knowledge from behavioural science to improve their decision-making, and to guide their own behaviours in ways that enrich their lives' (ibid.: 4).

This framework of governance, and the focus on the ways in which government can influence the 'choice architecture' of the social environment in which individuals take decisions, fundamentally challenges the traditional liberal assumptions on which the division of the public and private spheres – the sphere of government policy-making and the sphere of individual freedom – were constructed.

Once the human subject is understood as lacking in the capacity to make 'free choices', the private sphere becomes problematized and 'life' becomes the subject of governance.[4] As Mark Duffield has highlighted, this discourse of resilience increasingly shifts the emphasis of security discourses from specific problems of the external world to the problematization of the inner world, and the inner capacities and capabilities of citizens (Duffield 2011).

Bringing in the inner world: Friedrich von Hayek and the psychology of the brain

For classical liberal framings of *Homo œconomicus*, the inside of the human head was as out of bounds as the inside of the sovereign state in international relations theory. Liberal frameworks of thought have always been vulnerable to critical deconstruction through the transgression of the disciplinary boundaries keeping apart the interior and the exterior worlds of the liberal subject. Many of the most radical of these critiques have come from within the sphere of economic theorizing, particularly the new institutionalist economic challenge to classical liberal assumptions of the smooth or natural operation of market rationality. These authors were keen to explain the problematic nature of market relations in terms of the cultural or ideational contexts in which the human mind operated. The critique of the rationalist assumptions of classical liberalism enabled a new programmatic of governance and societal resilience to emerge in response to the unknowability and unpredictability of the external world. In this framing of the human subject, both individually and collectively, the problematic becomes one of adaptation and resilience: how individuals and societies respond to a shifting external environment is prioritized over and against conceptions of the state as capable of planning, directing or controlling socio-economic affairs (see Hayek 1960; Foucault 2008: 171–4).

As John R. Commons described new institutional economics back in 1936, it is based on understanding the importance of cultural and ideational contexts of choice-making – 'man's relationship to man' – ignored in classical liberal economic theory 'based on man's relation to nature' (1936: 242). For Commons, the intangibles, such as goodwill, conceptions of rights and duties, etc., all influenced the 'reasonable' price that the buyer was willing to pay. These intangibles were understood to be shaped by collective institutions and collective norms and controls, which meant that the classic liberal assumptions of perfect competition did not exist. Commons suggested that there was a 'nationalistic theory of value': that these national collective institutions meant that it was a fiction to think of the market as universalist in its operation; as much of a fiction as the belief in the universal individual subject of classical liberal political and economic theory:

> Even the individual of economic theory is not the natural individual of biology and psychology: he is that artificial bundle of institutes known as a legal person, or citizen. He is made such by sovereignty which grants to him the rights and liberties to buy and sell, borrow and lend, hire and hire out, work and not work, on his own free will. Merely as an individual of classical and hedonistic theory he is a factor of production and consumption like a cow or slave. Economic theory should make him a citizen, or member of the institution under whose rule he acts. (Ibid.: 247–8)

The paragraph above sums up the essence of societal resilience, which frees the individual from the strictures of classic liberal assumptions, allowing autonomy of choices but only once the individual is understood as a product of an institutional framework, a subject of their 'choice environment'. Commons therefore stressed that rather than treating humans as automatic pursuers of fixed interests, real-life behaviour had to be understood as shaped by institutional forms, especially those of custom and social norms (Forest and Mehier 2001). The individual will acted through conscious rational choice but was also a product of historical and social embeddedness: shaped and constructed on the basis of existing norms and values (ibid.: 593).

The work of Commons and other new institutionalist economists was developed further by Herbert Simon, who directly challenged the assumptions of the rational decision-making capacity of the classical liberal subject, dethroning *Homo œconomicus* from economic rational choice theory. In his argument, there was no such thing as perfect information or perfect rationality, merely 'bounded rationality', where not all the facts could be known or all the possible options considered. The decisions made with 'bounded rationality' were made on the basis of a freely willed conscious choice but they no longer necessarily resulted in furthering the collective good or in optimal outcomes. This critique of the rationality of the liberal subject forms a crucial component of the governance programme of societal resilience, which recognizes and simultaneously problematizes the decision-making autonomy of the subject.

For the advocates of societal resilience, the work of Herbert Simon, particularly the articulation of 'bounded rationality', allows the critique of the liberal subject to operate without appearing to be overtly elitist or undemocratic. As Charlie Edwards suggests, this is not an overt critique of democratic assumptions of the rational subject per se but of the late-modern subject's capacity to deal with new, unexpected, exceptional or complex events. *Resilient Nation* argues that people who seem to be rational in everyday life 'may revert to irrational behaviour, especially in response to a specific risk' (2009: 41). The problematic of 'bounded rationality' suggests that societal resilience will fail if it focuses on specific risks, which people may have little understanding of or relationship to. The inculcation of resilience, in fact, depends on the abstraction from specific risks, to become a mode of life, a way of social being: 'Risk communication cannot be detached from our everyday lives. It has to be hotwired into our decision-making processes and behaviours' (ibid.: 43). In making resilience a matter of the 'everyday', the exceptional event becomes essential to our understanding of and construction of new norms of decision-making and state–society relations.

The crucial facet of new institutionalist economics was that differences in responses to external shocks or unusual events could be understood as conscious, subjective choices, rather than as structurally imposed outcomes. The important research focus was then the individual making the decisions and the subjectively created institutional frameworks (formal and informal) determining or structuring these choices. This is a social perspective which starts from the individual as a decision-maker and then works outwards to understand why 'wrong' or problematic responses to events occur. In this perspective the individual subject is understood in isolation from their structuring social and economic context. 'Wrong' choices are understood first in terms of ideational blockages at the level of culture, custom or ideology and in terms of the formal institutional blockages – the 'choice architecture' or the incentives and opportunities available to enable other choices. This problematization of the individual shares much with therapeutic approaches, which also work at the level of the resilience of the individual (attempting to remove psychological blockages to making better choices) rather than at the level of social or economic relations (see, for example, Neenan 2009; Reivich and Shatte 2003; Clarke and Nicholson 2010) and, of course, it is from psychology that, as we examine later, Giddens takes the conception of the 'autotelic self' (see Nakamura and Csikszentmihalyi 2009).

The leading theorist of the inversion of state–society relations and responsibilities was Austrian economist Friedrich von Hayek, whose ideas have become central to agent-centred understandings of societal security and resilience (see, for example, Walker and Cooper 2011). Writing in the 1950s, Hayek was concerned that liberal universalist teleologies of socio-economic progress would lead to the dominance of socialist or communist frameworks of government. In order to combat this, Hayek sought to reintroduce difference as ontologically prior to universality and to flag up the internal limits to subjective reasoning. Perhaps his most insightful work in this area is *The Sensory Order: An Inquiry into the Foundations of Theoretical Psychology* (1952). As the title indicates, for Hayek the key area in which limits were to be located was in the psychological make-up of the subject.

For Marx, the key attribute of the human was the ability to imagine an end or goal before carrying it out – the capacity, through reason, to subordinate the self to an external object of transformation – to consciously transform the world through a self-directed aim (1954: 174).[5] Hayek, on the other hand, was interested in the hold of the past and the incapacity of the subject to cope with the external world because reasoning could be based only on the way that individual ways of thinking are predicated upon past experiences. Our minds build models and expectations based on previous experiences which mean that our behavioural responses depend less on the 'reality' we are confronted with than on the psychological preconditioning of our minds. Our consciousness, in fact, prevents us from engaging with the world in a rational way (1952: 25). For Hayek:

> Like many of the traditional schools of psychology, behaviouralism thus treated the problem of mind as if it were a problem of the responses of the individual to an independently or objectively given phenomenal world; while in fact it is the existence of a phenomenal world which is different from the physical world which constitutes the main problem. (Ibid.: 28)

Hayek's focus on the mind of the subject enabled him to remove the external world as an object of universalist understanding: in effect, he argued that the external world was merely a subjectivist phenomenological product. It therefore followed that it was not the external world of social relations which produced and reproduced difference and hierarchy but the internal differences of the human brain. The problem was not that we are not rational or 'enlightened' enough to understand the external world, but that the external world appears only through the phenomenological constructions of our minds. These phenomenologies are the products of 'interpretations' based upon inherited and learned experiences which mediate between the experience and the response: 'we cannot hope to account for observed behaviour without reconstructing the "intervening processes in the brain"' (ibid.: 44). It is our cognitive processes which make us respond differently to our external environments and can help explain different developmental outcomes which reproduce the same experiences and response mechanisms. Internal differentiations therefore are reproduced and exaggerate our differential responses to events, particularly unfamiliar ones.

In Hayek's work, we see not only how psychological explanations begin to play a larger role in understanding the importance of practices of societal resilience but also how responses to security risks or threats can be reinterpreted in terms of the environmental influence on the workings of the brain. Cognitive processes are complex, integrated networks, but they are also malleable and capable of adaptive change, depending upon the extent to which 'phylogenetic', inherited patterns and connections, and 'ontogenetic' aspects, acquired by the individual during the course of their lifetime, interact (ibid.: 80–1). Where Marx sharply distinguished the human from the natural world, Hayek's focus on the psychology of the brain focuses on how human responses are shaped through resilience and adaption, in ways which are little different to those of any other living organism:

> The continued existence of those complex structures which we call organisms is made possible by their capacity of responding to certain external influences by such changes in their structure or activity as are required to maintain or restore the balance necessary for their persistence. (Ibid.: 82)

Individuals, especially more complex organisms like humans, will respond differently to external stimuli in ways which enable them to discriminate differently between different stimuli and to react differently. Often these differences will not be intentional but arbitrary or accidental. The key point for Hayek is that differential experiences and reactions necessarily result from the innate historical experiential differences of individuals and their different internal (rather than external) environments: 'one of the most important parts of the "environment" from which the central nervous system will receive signals producing linkages, will be the *milieu intérieur*, the internal environment or the rest of the organism in which the central nervous system exists' (ibid.: 109).

Hayek inverts the liberal framework of the autonomous and rational subject, capable of transforming the external world, through asserting that liberal frameworks and institutions are necessary precisely because the liberal subject is not capable of knowing or transforming the external world. The progressive impulse of liberalism appears exhausted in this defence of liberal modernity on the basis that democracy and markets work best because this enables us to adapt and to cope with problems without the possibility of knowledge or control. In effect, this reduces human collectives to the ontological status of biological organisms, merely capable of adaptation through evolutionary chance rather than through conscious decision-making. Of course, it is here, in the defence of liberalism on the basis of the inability of the subject to shape or control an external world, that the discursive practices of societal resilience become a necessity rather than an option.

In terms of genealogical framings, it is important to emphasize that what is key in the work of early new institutional economics, and developed further in the ideas of Hayek, is a conceptual framework critiquing classical liberal assumptions. This critique was based upon the decentring of the human subject as a rational agent, capable of securing itself through knowing and shaping its external environment. Many aspects of today's human-centred discourses of community resilience are present in this construction of the subject in relation to the problematic of its adaptation to its external world. However, the context in which these concerns were articulated was one very different to our own. The chief concern was that of a defence of liberal frameworks of rule against the backdrop of socio-economic crisis and the challenge of socialist or communist alternatives, which stressed the potential of human agency to shape and control events through abolishing or restricting market relations. It took the defeat of the radical mass movements, which challenged the market system, before the articulation of human reasoning as a barrier to change could be represented as a progressive, even radical, framework of social empowerment. The next section considers how the exhaustion of liberalism and the hollowing out of the liberal subject has been articulated anew as a governing programme in our 'globalized', insecure and 'post-political' world.

Removing the outer world: Anthony Giddens and manufactured uncertainty

In order to contextualize the inner logic of discourses of societal resilience, I have traced some guidelines of resilience genealogically through the economic theories which stressed the internal world of the decision-making subject as constituting the key barrier to societal security. The discursive importance of the internal world of the subject, however, played a relatively marginal role in mainstream liberal social theorizing as a programme of government. It was only in the post-Cold War era that discourses of security, both broadly and narrowly defined, shifted to societal rather than state based approaches. Today, it is clear in discourses of societal resilience that what was once a marginal preoccupation has now become central to understanding the world we live in and the role of the state in relation to society. As Foucault highlighted, in his work on the birth of biopolitics (focusing on the exceptional circumstances of the post-war West German state), the governing of the social involves a shift from a focus on the state provision of the means of security to the internal capacities of individuals in civil society, understood to be potentially problematic decision-making subjects (2008). It could be argued that Foucault's work in this area was highly prescient, to the extent that today it appears that the shift to divesting security responsibility to society, and with this the shift to concern over the internal world of the individual, means that the external world could be said to no longer exist in a meaningful way for us.[6]

Anthony Giddens has been one of the most articulate advocates of the shift from the external to the internal world and in turning this into an activist and proactive programme of governance in the wake of the collapse of left/right framings of liberal modernity in the post-Cold War period. In his 1990s work *Beyond Left and Right* (1994) and on *The Third Way* (1998; see also 2000) he clearly articulated the shift from the liberal modernist belief that developments in science and technology might enable the extension of humanity's control over the external world: that 'human beings can become not just authors but the masters of their own destiny' (1994: 3). He argued that today we have become aware that the aspiration of controlling and shaping our external world was a product of human hubris and misunderstanding. Today's globalized world is a dislocated, uncertain, insecure, 'runaway world'. What is more:

> disturbingly, what was supposed to create greater and greater certainty – the advance of human knowledge and 'controlled intervention' into society and nature – is actually deeply involved with this unpredictability ... The uncertainties thus created I shall refer to generically as *manufactured uncertainty*. (Ibid.: 3–4)

These uncertainties and insecurities, because they are conceived of as human products (or by-products), cannot be dealt with through Enlightenment prescriptions of 'more knowledge, more control' (ibid.: 4) but rather through coming to terms with the need to limit and rethink our understanding of humanity's relationship with the external world. The problem, for Giddens, is the indirect nature of our relationship to our environment. For him, globalization can best be described as 'action at a distance' (ibid.: 4): globalization – the complexity and interconnectedness of our world – means that our actions have effects at a distance from their intended effects and that similarly we are affected by the actions of others, despite their intentions. In other words, what we do has global effects upon our own security, although we cannot see or predict what these may be.

For Giddens, societal resilience becomes the sphere of intelligibility for both the problems and insecurities faced by collective humanity and for the development of frameworks for governing this uncertainty. The compulsion towards resilience-based framings of the world stems from the asserted exhaustion of the Enlightenment project: the rejection of the cosy meanings and understandings which liberal modernity imposed on the world at the alleged cost of the agency and freedom of the human subject:

> Today we must break with providentialism, in whatever guise it might present itself. Not for us the idea that capitalism is pregnant with socialism. Not for us the idea that there is a historical agent –

whether proletariat or any other – that will more or less automatically come to our rescue. Not for us the idea that 'history' has any necessary direction at all. We must accept risk as risk, up to and including the most potentially cataclysmic of high-consequence risks; we must accept that there can be no way back to external risk from manufactured risk. (Ibid.: 249)

The key point to grasp from Giddens's framework is that our decisions or our choices have much broader and more powerful consequences than we can imagine. The logical consequence is that our world becomes seen and understood as a product of our individual choices. For Giddens there is no outside to humanity conceived of as choice-making individuals. There is no external world of structures and social relations or of natural laws open to discovery (already prefigured in his earlier work on structuration theory; see 1984; for its relation to social constructivism see Berger and Luckmann 1979). We have globalized our own world, consigning the world of the Enlightenment or of liberal modernity to the history books. The liberal world presupposed an external world open to our understanding and therefore to our manipulation and control (as discussed in the previous chapter). There can be no Cartesian subject without an outside and no Cartesian teleology of progress. Giddens describes the disappearance of the external world in terms of the 'disappearance of nature, where "nature" refers to environments and events given independently of human action' (1994: 6). Nothing exists outside our actions and consequently our actions are everything. If there is a problem to be addressed the only sphere of engagement can be with the sphere of human action, understood as the decisional choices of individuals.

As Giddens states: 'Manufactured uncertainty intrudes into all the arenas of life thus opened up to decision-making' (ibid.: 6). The world is reduced to individual decision-making and at the same time individual decision-making becomes the sphere of policy-making activity. The reason for this is that we discover that there are major problems with the individual decision-makers: human beings. We are not equipped to exist in a world which is dependent on our decision-making capacities. Where the fixed structures and certainties no longer operate we are forced to pay particular attention to how we make decisions; as we increasingly shape our own lives, we deploy 'social reflexivity' and are in danger of increasing the problems which we ourselves are confronted with. 'The growth of social reflexivity is a major factor introducing a dislocation between knowledge and control – a prime source of manufactured uncertainty' (ibid.: 7).

For Giddens, the problem is that at a time when we have to make more decisions than ever before, and the consequences of our individual decision-making are of global consequence, we come up against a major barrier. This barrier is an internal one – the way in which our brains work. We are not well equipped to deal with complex autonomy and so we need external assistance. This is where the work of Giddens develops and expands upon the work of the new institutionalist economists considered above, transforming this conceptual defence of liberalism into a programme of governance intervention (see also, for example, North 1990, 2005). The development of governance 'choice-shaping' to assist us in our autonomous choice-making Giddens calls 'generative politics'. The state can no longer do things for us in a directive and controlling way and so must confront the urgent and complex task of empowering the subject to make better life choices:

> Generative politics is a politics which seeks to allow individuals and groups to make things happen, rather than have things happen to them, in the context of overall social concerns and goals ... it does not situate itself in the old opposition between state and market. It works through providing material conditions, and organisational frameworks, for the life-political decisions taken by individuals and groups in the wider social order. (1994: 15)

This focus on the inner life of the subject rather than on the state as a director of society, as Giddens himself notes, owes much to the work of Friedrich Hayek, who similarly critiqued the 'cybernetic model' of a controlling and knowing state. In fact, it is the lack of knowledge of a complex and globalized world which necessitates the focus on the individual rather than the state. For Giddens, this shift takes on full force only in late modernity with the complexity of society. While top-down decision-making might work for early modernizing states, in a world of globalization and high reflexivity only bottom-up decision-making enables the high level of reflexivity and adaptability required for societal security. The focus on the inner life of the individual highlights the conceptual core of societal resilience's rejection of liberal frameworks of social order and its drive to divest securing power. As Edwards states:

Community resilience requires an altogether more nuanced and subtle approach that is premised on institutions and organisations letting go, creating the necessary framework for action, rather than developing specific plans and allowing community resilience to emerge and develop in local areas over time. No single plan exists, never should and hopefully never will. The role of central government in community resilience will always be limited. It will not be the main protagonist, a supporting actor or an extra – rather its role will be played out behind the scenes by a supporting cast of players who ensure the system is operating to the best of its ability. Adopting this invisible role will not be easy for central government. (2009: 80)

The external world has disappeared in two interconnected ways (as discussed in the previous chapter). First, it is unknowable, it is globalized: the relations of cause and effect no longer appear to operate clearly because we have lost control over the consequences of our actions. The unintended effects overwhelm the intended ones because the world is much more complicated and interconnected than we imagined in liberal teleologies of progress and control. Secondly, the external world disappears because we can no longer distinguish ourselves from the world. In the words of Anthony Giddens, there is no longer any external 'nature' – our external world has been shaped by human actions and choices but not conscious ones. Not only is the world unknowable, it is unknowable because it is a human world.

While it is a human world, it is not thereby a liberal world as we knew it: the external world has been closed off to us and with it there can be no universal framing bringing us together on the basis of human beings as transforming subjects. Work on the transformation of the internal world of post-liberal subjects can understand the subject only as increasingly differentiated in its choice-making vulnerability, rather than as a potential collectivity. In this respect, the universalizing discourse of post-liberalism, which is inclusive in its emphasis on our shared nature as vulnerable subjects, is one which can operate only within and upon discourses of societal resilience, continually 'learning' that the most vulnerable are those most in need of empowering in order to cope with uncertainty and risk.

There is still a discourse of transformation but it is not about the transformation of the external world but the ongoing process of transforming the inner world of individuals. As the UK Cabinet Office's *Strategic National Framework on Community Resilience* suggests: 'This programme is part of the Government's "Big Society" commitment to reduce the barriers which prevent people from being able to help themselves and to become more resilient to shocks' (2011b: 3). Societal security is understood to depend on the social empowerment of individuals whose securing agency is held back by the wrong institutional 'choice-shaping' or cultural and ideational frameworks:

> The Government contribution to community resilience is not to dictate or measure what is being or should be done locally. Instead, the role is to support and enable local activity by making existing good practice available to others who are interested, and removing the barriers and debunking the myths which prevent communities from taking local action. (Ibid.: 7)

Giddens clearly articulates the project of societal empowerment as the development of the autonomy of the individual. The internalized nature of the project is clear in the emphasis upon the modern subject's need for 'self-help' and 'self-construction':

> The advance of social reflexivity means that individuals have no choice but to make choices; and these choices define who they are. People have to 'construct their own biographies' in order to sustain a coherent sense of self-identity. (1994: 126)

Humans may not be able to 'master their own destiny' but, for Giddens, they need to 'construct their own biographies'. Giddens's work is very important for understanding and drawing out the consequences of an internalized conception of security within discourses of resilience and its relationship to our understanding of the human subject. One way in which he illustrates the shift is in our understanding of the threats to societal security. In the pre-liberal age, or pre-Enlightenment era, the main conceptual framework was that of fate or nature or God – catastrophic events could not be prevented, merely accepted. In the liberal era, the dominant framework of understanding was that of 'risk' or 'accident', something that highlighted the borders of control and could be calculated, minimized or insured against. The point being that 'accidents' or 'risks' were conceptualized as external factors, outside control. Giddens argues that today there is no outside, no external area, no external risk. Once the problem is understood in terms of manufactured risk, setbacks and damage, as a consequence of the decisions we take ourselves, work on the self is the only area through which these problems can be addressed.

A good example Giddens gives to demonstrate the difference between an external risk and an internal one is the changing nature of health security, shifting from intervention to prevention. In the liberal world, we understood that there was a risk of getting cancer or other ailments in old age and the attempt to address the problem was in the development of medicine and forms of diagnosis and interventionist treatment. In the post-liberal world, Giddens advocates a different approach of prevention based on the inculcation of resilience, of work on the self: changing attitudes and social norms to empower individuals to make better life-choices and adopt better lifestyle habits. Societal security through resilience is understood as empowering, as liberating the agency of the individual. Another example is Giddens's view of old age: 'Aging is treated as "external", as something that happens to one, not as a phenomenon actively constructed and negotiated' (ibid.: 170). Giddens seeks to argue that old age is a matter of individual choice: 'many of the physical difficulties of old age are not to do with aging at all, but rather with lifestyle practices' (ibid.: 170). Rather than understanding cancer as an externality, which should be provided for by government health and welfare services, the agent-centred approach of societal resilience increasingly understands health problems as the production of the individual subject itself. The increasing scientific dominance of this approach is highlighted by the scientific support for the recent Cancer UK research report which asserts that over 40 per cent of cancers are caused by lifestyle choices, including choices regarding smoking, drinking alcohol, salt intake, the consumption of red meat, body weight, regular exercise and exposure to sun and sunbeds (Parkin 2011; also Roberts 2011). Where the Enlightenment philosophers, such as Condorcet, imagined that the external-oriented growth of science and technology could lead to expansions of the human lifespan well beyond 100 years (Condorcet 2009 [1795]), experts in societal resilience assert that the same can be achieved through internal growth and care of the self.

The key point made by advocates of resilience approaches is that societal security has to be addressed at the level of the inner life or the inner capacities of the individual rather than the material level. This transformation occurs through recognizing the importance of individual agency and establishing a proactive relationship to potentially destabilizing security risks:

> Schemes of positive welfare, orientated to manufactured rather than external risk, would be directed to fostering the *autotelic self*. The autotelic self is one with an inner confidence which comes from self-respect, and one where a sense of ontological security, originating in basic trust, allows for a positive appreciation of social difference. It refers to a person able to translate potential threats into rewarding challenges, someone who is able to turn entropy into a consistent flow of experience. The autotelic self does not seek to neutralize risk or to suppose that 'someone else will take care of the problem'; *risk is confronted as the active challenge which generates self-actualization*. (Giddens 1994: 192, emphasis added)

Giddens, in effect, generates a programme of agent-centred transformation on the basis of the unknowability and the contingency of the external world. This programme is a transformative one, but the object of transformation is the inner life of the individual: the project to 'foster the autotelic self'. The autotelic self is understood as an individual capable of self-governing in a world of contingency and radical uncertainty. The autotelic self turns insecurity into self-actualization, into growth. It is very different from the universalized subject of liberal modernity. Whereas the modern liberal subject was assumed to have the will and capacity to act on and to transform, to secure and to know its external world, the transformative activity of the autotelic self is restricted to the internal realm.

Choice and the human subject

The exclusion of the external world, in the discourses of resilience and societal security both results in and reflects the removal of a whole raft of social, economic and political concerns from public political contestation. Hannah Arendt acutely warned of just such a shift to the private realm, where the emphasis is on the transformation of behaviour rather than a focus on the active transformation of the external world. She argued that this perspective would abolish the world of political struggle and reduce the state and government purely to administration (1998: 45). Perhaps more importantly, Arendt powerfully challenged the ideological implication of choice-based theorization, that, in the words of Giddens, we can 'be authors of our own biographies':

> Although everybody started his life by inserting himself into the
> human world through action and speech, nobody is the author
> or producer of his own life story. In other words, the stories, the
> results of action and speech, reveal an agent, but this agent is not
> an author or producer. Somebody began it and is its subject in
> the twofold sense of the word, namely, its actor and sufferer, but
> nobody is its author. (Ibid.: 184)

In the transition away from the external to the inner world, what humanity has in common is no longer the external world (which we can individually and collectively subordinate to our conscious will) but the inner world, the structure of our minds (ibid.: 283). From Arendt's insights, we can argue that the essence of institutionalist or societal approaches to resilience is their reduction of the public or social world to the inner world of psychological processes. The social, collective, plural mediation of the world (as human artefact) no longer acts as a 'table', relating and separating us, enabling us to constitute the human as a collective, plural, active and transformative subject (ibid.: 52–3).

The key point, for those of us concerned with developing an understanding and critique of agent-centred discourses and practices of societal resilience and work on the inner self, is that 'freedom' and 'choice' are entirely degraded once the world is reduced to the inner life of the individual. In making choice- and decision-making the moment of understanding and of policy intervention, freedom is made subordinate to external necessity. When the UK Cabinet Office, Giddens or new institutionalist economists talk of 'choices' they are degrading the concept of choice along with the formal autonomy of the liberal subject. Here choice is reduced to responsibility. There is no genuine choice-making, merely the allocation of blame, on the basis that as we are responsible for our decisions and choices; our inner lives are thereby open to external judgement and intervention. This discourse is universal, enabling us to understand the 'poor choice-making', or the lack of societal resilience, of our fellow citizens and neighbours, if they happen to be unemployed, to smoke, to be teenage mothers, eat fatty food, drop litter, fail to take up higher education opportunities or to properly handle their emotions. The reduction of social, economic, political and environmental questions to ones of individual choice-making capacities is so pervasive we often do not give the broader discourses of resilience a second thought.

The telos of tracing authorship of the world to individual choice-making removes the freedom to make choices: every point of choice-making becomes a point of potential judgement, a point of explanation and a point of governance intervention. What, for Arendt, made the human creative and transformative – the fact that our actions are unbounded as other autonomous humans react to them and others to their acts – becomes an argument for limitations; an argument to explain and rationalize societal insecurities and to justify the imposition of regulatory control. For Althusser, as for Arendt:

> That human, i.e. social individuals are active in history – as agents … – that is a fact. But, considered as agents, human individuals are not 'free' and 'constitutive' subjects in the philosophical sense of these terms. They work in and through the determinations of the forms of historical existence of the social relations of production and reproduction (labour process, division and organization of labour, process of production and reproduction, class struggle, etc.). (2008: 134)

The discourses of societal resilience insist that our responsibility be expanded beyond legal frameworks of regulation, insisting that 'lifestyle choices' can be securitized and thus open to regulative intervention and 'choice-shaping'.

Conclusion

In essence, discourses of societal resilience seek to extend the responsibility of individuals to the future consequences of their unbounded actions: to the social relations in which they act and decide. Discourses of resilience cast the post-liberal subject as the autotelic self, asserting that the barriers to safe and secure 'reflexive' decision-making need to be removed by government 'choice-shaping', designed to free us as securing and self-governing subjects through the development of our inner capacities and capabilities. The programme of societal resilience is based on the transformation of the inner life of the subject to facilitate better choice-making; concomitant with this is the denial of the reasoned moral autonomy of the subject and the subordination of choice-making to external necessity.

Our freedom to autonomously decide is taken away at the same time as the material constraints of our social relations become recast in terms of the social and environmental influences on our cognitive processes. Capitalism is naturalized and normalized at the same time as human rationality is degraded and denied. The problem for societal resilience is always the human rather than the social relations in which humans are embedded. The governance practices aimed at societal resilience and the construction of resilient communities rely upon the collapsing of the external world into the interior of the human head. This collapsing of the material relations of the external world into the intersubjective contexts of cognition is essential to the agent- or human-centred frameworks of understanding. This process will be drawn out further in the following chapter, extending the discussion from the sphere of security to that of development. In the shift from understanding development as a question of transforming the external world to a question of the subject's inner capabilities, transformative change becomes fully a matter of work on the self.

4 | DEVELOPMENT AND HUMAN AGENCY

Introduction

Development in the human-centred problematic has little to do with transforming the conditions of the external world. Therefore development does not refer as much to material things or products as to the individual capacities to undertake the necessary actions and decisions. Under the agent-centred understanding, in which there is no contingency of social structures between individuals and the world, the problem of development can be addressed only at the level of the actions and choice-making capacities of the poorest and most marginal sections of society. In the words of Martha Nussbaum, for example: 'poverty is best understood as capability failure, not just as shortage of commodities or even of income and wealth' (Nussbaum 2011: 143). The active policy of societal intervention, whether posed as interventions within domestic society or considered more broadly as a set of policy interventions to address vulnerabilities on an international scale, is oriented around the development of the human subject itself. In this discourse, societal intervention with the goal of transforming the subject introduces the understanding of necessity into the realm of individual choice-making.

As will be considered in this chapter, the discourse of developing adaptive capabilities and capacities removes the traditional government policy goals previously associated with state-led development policy-making. Whereas liberal frameworks of governmentality focused upon how governments might regulate and control specific levers of the economy – inflation levels, unemployment rates, interest rates, etc. – under human-centred approaches, the government of economic processes (now reduced to administrative and technical expertise) becomes much less important than the understanding of societal processes, particularly those societal processes concerning the internal capacities of individuals, enabling them to make better lifestyle choices. Recasting development in terms of societal processes and the problematic of individual choice-making removes poverty and inequality from the macro or state level of policy-making. Rather than being addressed through macroeconomic policy-making, based on government programmes and goals, development becomes a societal problem. The liberal programmatic of government becomes hollowed out as liberal economic policy goals are displaced by the societal goal of social 'empowerment' or 'capability-building'. In these agent-centred understandings, governments have no economic or developmental goals beyond enlarging the sphere of individual adaptive capabilities, often presented in terms of 'human development'.

In development discourses, the building of agential capacity is often understood in terms of Amartya Sen's formulation of 'development as freedom' (1999). In this framework, the subject becomes incrementally 'free' through the development of choice-making capabilities. This chapter seeks to explore how concepts of development, freedom and capacity-building operate in a distinct way in these human-centred approaches. In liberal modernity, freedom was the presupposition for the subject's autonomy and rights ownership. However, in the continuum of agent-centred approaches, adaptive capacities are always under development: in this sense the subject of human-centred development is never understood as 'free' but always in the process of enlarging or developing its freedom under necessity, understood in terms of adaptive capacity.

This chapter engages with the agent-centred discourses of capability- and capacity-building through reference to Foucault's critical exploration of shifts and transformations in liberal frameworks of understanding the role of government. Here, Foucault's work is very insightful in highlighting how our understanding of the human subject has been transformed within agent-centred development discourses. In today's dominant conceptualization of human-centred approaches to development, human agency has been placed at the centre and is increasingly seen to be the measure of development, in terms of individual adaptive capacities. The individualized understanding of development removes the mediating understanding of contingency. There is no gap between the individual and the world. The individual is in the world but without any social relations mediating the actions and choices of the individual and the effects of these choices and actions as they appear in the world. This view of the individual as the creator of the world – of the individual as responsible for the world – can start the analysis of the world only from the individual subject itself. In this analysis, the world becomes entirely a construct of the agential actions and choices of the individual, and therefore it is termed the 'agent-centred' or 'the agent-orientated view' (ibid.: 11). This chapter therefore critically engages with the view of human action and choice-making as constitutive of the world and of the problematic understanding of human agency which must necessarily be articulated within this approach.

In this discourse, development is taken out of an economic context of GDP growth or industrial modernization, or a social and political context, in which development policies are shaped by social and political pressures or state-led policies. Foucault's work on the disappearance or invisibility of power, particularly as articulated through the shift towards what he understood as agent-centred frameworks, focusing on the irreducible decision-making subject – 'the rationality of the governed' (2008: 312) – will be used to critically engage with Sen and other theorists of the 'capabilities approach'. This chapter genealogically draws out the changing nature of Western discourses of development and the understanding of policy practices as promoting the empowerment of the post-colonial other in order to examine how development and autonomy have been radically differently articulated in discourses of Western power and how today's discursive framing feeds on and transforms colonial and early post-colonial approaches to the human subject.

In today's agent-centred framings, human agency is at the heart of development discourse. This centrality of the human is often greeted as liberating and emancipatory in contrast to the framings of liberal modernity, which are alleged to see economic growth as a matter of material richness. The work of Nobel Prize-winning economist Amartya Sen has been central in establishing the conceptual foundations of the human development discourse underpinning today's dominant understanding of development and to the establishment of the United Nations Development Programme's annual *Human Development* reports and Human Development Index. Here, it is the growth of human capabilities which is central: the empowerment of the individual. In fact, as Martha Nussbaum notes, this approach is often more usefully termed the 'Capabilities Approach' (Nussbaum 2011: x). Development is taken out of a macro socio-economic context and seen as a question of individual inclusion and choice-making capabilities.

The first annual United Nations Human Development Report (1990) opens with these paragraphs:

This Report is about people – and about how development enlarges their *choices*. It is about more than GNP growth, more than income and wealth and more than producing commodities and accumulating capital. A person's access to income may be one of the *choices*, but it is not the sum total of human endeavour.

Human development is a process of enlarging people's *choices*. The most critical of these wide-ranging *choices* are to live a long and healthy life, to be educated and to have access to resources needed for a decent standard of living. Additional *choices* include political freedom, guaranteed human rights and personal self-respect.

Development enables people to have these *choices*. No one can guarantee human happiness, and the *choices* people make are their own concern. But the process of development should at least create a conducive environment for people, individually and collectively, to develop their full potential and to have a reasonable chance of leading productive and creative lives in accord with their needs and interests.

Human development thus concerns more than the formation of human capabilities, such as improved health or knowledge. It also concerns the use of these capabilities, be it for work, leisure or political and cultural activities. And if the scales of human development fail to balance the formation and use of human capabilities, much human potential will be frustrated. (UNDP 1990: 1, emphasis added)

The seven occasions on which the word 'choices' is used in the first three paragraphs have been italicized in order to emphasize that human development is inextricably tied to the extension of choice-making capabilities. The key point to note is that these capabilities are disconnected from the level of material social and economic development; as the third and fourth paragraphs emphasize, choice-making capability is thereby disconnected from the external environment seen as providing resources for the exercise of capabilities. There is a large internal or subjective element to the capability approach – the concern is with 'the use of these capabilities' and with the 'conducive environment' in which good choice-making can take place.

There has been a lot of academic and technical discussion over the merits and applicability of Sen's approach, which has generally sought to expand Sen's framework rather than to critically engage with it (for a good summary, see Clark 2005). When Sen has been the subject of criticism, this has generally focused on the need for collective political struggle to constitute development and freedom for the post-colonial subject or for paying too little attention to the structural constraints of the world market and capitalist social relations (see, for example, Navarro 2000; Samaddar 2006; Chimni 2008; Harvey 2005: 184). The human development capabilities approach has also been substantially critiqued from a traditional development perspective for the shift away from material definitions of development to a more subjective measurement (see, for example, Pender 2001; Ben-Ami 2006; Duffield 2007; Pupavac 2007). Mark Duffield's work is emblematic in this respect, and he highlights the problematic of development as a technology of liberal governance in his influential book *Development, Security and Unending War* (2007):

> Sustainable development is about creating diversity and choice, enabling people to manage the risks and contingencies of their existence better and, through regulatory and disciplinary interventions, helping surplus population to maintain a homeostatic condition of self-reliance. (Ibid.: 115)

This chapter seeks to mount a different engagement with Sen's work, instead taking seriously the claim of 'development as freedom' to explore Sen's re-reading of development as the inculcation of individual capacities. Rather than see adaptive capacity-building as a technology of liberal governmentality, it seeks instead to consider Sen's work in a broader context of the understanding of the human subject itself; particularly as it is articulated at the limits of liberalism and helps to construct and shape these limits – in terms of the problematization of the colonial and post-colonial subject.

It will be suggested that Foucault, following Marx, powerfully theorizes the problematic of the shifts and transformations within liberal thought as the liberal project increasingly exhausts the emancipatory potential of the Enlightenment.[1] These shifts are incrementally reflected in the shrinking of the liberal world and in the reduction of the liberal understanding of the subject, as barriers and limits are increasingly introduced, at first as external and then as internal to the human subject. For Foucault, the shifting understanding of the human subject was of crucial importance: his work on biopolitics and the government of the self can be read as a critical engagement with understanding the reshaping of liberal aspirations from a concern with the knowledge of and transformation of the external world to the management of the inner world of subjects, articulated clearly in the shift from government, based upon liberal frames of representation, to agent-centred governance, the regulation of societal processes. In this shift, our understanding of what it means to be human, and of what being human means for our engagement with the world we live in, has been fundamentally altered.

Foucault deals with this problematic on several occasions, most notably in his work on *The Birth of Biopolitics* (2008) but also through analogy in his study of the decay of Greek democratic thought, especially as reflected in the work of Plato (2010). While Foucault engaged critically with this shift, I want to suggest that the work of Amartya Sen provides a good example of the power of agent- or human-centred understandings. Sen's conception of 'development as freedom' inverts classical or traditional framings of both these terms and shifts the emphasis of both problematics to the inner world of the subject. In fact, development disappears – it has no external material measurement – it is deontologized, or rather assumes the ontology of the human subject itself. At the same time, freedom is also dissolved as a meaningful way of understanding the political or legal status of the subject: freedom also loses its materiality as it loses its external universalist moorings and instead becomes relocated to the interior life of the individual.

Foucault's work on the genealogy of the subject

In *The Birth of Biopolitics*, Foucault drew out the implications of agent-centred approaches and was very keen to highlight the limitation of the left or Marxist thinking of his day, which emphasized, in the shift from state- to society-based policy-making, the rolling back of the state and the expansion of market forces, with the increased emphasis on the self-reliance and the responsibilization of the subject (which critical work by both Marx- and Foucault-inspired theorists, such as David Harvey and Mark Duffield, seems to replicate today) (2008: 129–50). Foucault focused upon the limits of understanding these discourses in largely economic terms, with the assumptions that their impact was mainly at the economic level and that they could be contested in terms of left versus right or the state versus the market. He argued that the rise of agent-centred discourses reflected a major shift in how politics could be understood or contested, and that this shift was entirely missed in traditional left/right polemics (ibid.: 116–17).

Foucault highlighted major shifts and transformations within liberal discourse, which made this transformation in the relationship between the subject and the state very different (ibid.: 118). He can be read as suggesting that discourses conceptualized here, in terms of agent-centred or post-liberal understandings, marked the shrinking of our understanding of human subjectivity, removing the foundational sphere of rational autonomy. In so doing, Foucault indicated that, with agent-centred approaches, the binaries of liberal thought were dissolved: that there was no longer a conceptual distinction between the external world and the inner world, between subject and object, between public and private, between the formal sphere of politics and law and the informal sphere of social and economic relations (ibid.: 267–86). There was no longer the universal starting position of the Enlightenment subject – capable of knowing and transforming the external world; of self-realization, of self-emancipation. There was no longer a liberal teleology of progress.

Foucault suggested that the focus upon the agency of the individual in the private societal sphere inverted our understanding of the human subject, at the same time making the internal life of the subject the subject of governance. Power and agency are reduced to the level of individual decision-taking. Individual decisions construct the world in which we live and shape the context for further decisions which individuals make. This world is continually being made and remade by the human subject. But the human subject here is not the classical subject of the Enlightenment: there is no assumption of growth in knowledge or understanding or progress. Effective governance can be seen only after the event on the basis of the outcomes of decisions; right or wrong choices cannot be established at the time. Government constantly needs to intervene to adapt institutions to enable better individual decisions, to work on the empowerment of the decision-making individual, or its adaptive capacities in the language of today's resilience-based theorizations. This is a continual process of preventive management of society based upon the indirect shaping of the capacities and conduct of its individual members (ibid.: 159–79).

Foucault spent his life working and reworking a genealogy of understanding the shifts in relations of government to the social sphere and the shrinking of the human subject through the reduction of the world to the inner life of the subject. The creation and the death or decline of the human subject and its relationship to the crisis of liberalism and of its forms of governing is a rich and engaging one. In *The Birth of Biopolitics* he considered whether the subjection of the subject – precisely through its capacity for subjective will – as a subject of individual choices which are both irreducible and non-transferable was already necessarily implied in the Enlightenment understanding of the subject or whether it was a contingent product of its economic and political development (ibid.: 271–3). This, of course, is a vital question for those of us interested in political alternatives which necessarily depend on a revitalized understanding of the Enlightenment subject or at least of how Enlightenment conceptions might have led to the subjective understandings of today.

In *The Government of the Self and Others* Foucault returned to this question. In going back to Immanuel Kant's *What is Enlightenment?* he suggested that despite the framework of self-emancipation, the Kantian project had an ambiguous approach to internal agency which facilitates and legitimizes the need for an external or outside agency which acts to 'free' the subject; in Kant's case the Enlightened monarch or, later, the French revolution (2010: 37–9). The call for the self-emancipation of the subject (considered as an autonomous individual) thereby implicitly allows for the possibility that those who have not emancipated themselves can be understood to lack their own agential capacity for choosing freedom and to require development through external agency to enable them to make better choices. Of most importance for the analysis presented here is that Foucault emphasized that for Kant the external agency does not 'free' the subject merely by removing external barriers to freedom.

The barrier to the Enlightenment of the individual is considered to be an internal one – the flaw of the subject is a matter of 'will' (ibid.: 29). The lack of freedom or autonomy is not due to external oppression or material deprivation, but 'a sort of deficit in the relationship of autonomy to oneself' (ibid.: 33). The King of Prussia or the Revolution does not act to 'free' the subject in the formal terms of liberation or self-government, but in enabling the subject to act according to reason and through enabling reason to guide choice-making. The fact that this is an inner problem means that subjugation or the lack of freedom is not a fixed, natural or inevitable product, and therefore introduces the possibility of transformation, but this framing also insists that the subject cannot be freed merely by the action of others – by ostensible or self-proclaimed 'liberators' (ibid.: 34). Foucault was keen to emphasize that Enlightenment as transformation/development is an internal matter of enabling the subject to free itself – to govern itself through reason.

Therefore, for Foucault, the Enlightenment subject was always one which was a potential subject of/for development understood as 'freedom' in similar terms to those articulated by new institutionalist economic theorists and international development agencies, which emphasize the need to capacity-build the individual subject today. Implicit within Enlightenment assumptions – hidden behind the autonomous subject – was a potential subject in need of governance: a subject which could establish the need for societal intervention and which could set the limits to external transformation or the resolution of societal problems through its own (lack of) development – understood as internal capacities for self-governance, will or adequate choice-making.[2] This framing is of vital importance to understand the discourse of 'development as freedom', as much as of other human-centred discourses, which talk of the development of autonomy, of self-realization, of empowerment and of vulnerability and resilience.

Foucault argued that while the liberal problematic always centred around the problematic of human reason and its limits, the human subject as a world-making subject could be understood only as a historical product of human struggle, rather than as a fixed or metaphysical construct (which we could construct in order to stand outside or 'oppose' the Enlightenment problematic):

> We must try to proceed with the analysis of ourselves as beings who are historically determined, to a certain extent, by the Enlightenment. Such an analysis implies a series of historical inquiries that are as precise as possible; and these inquiries will not be oriented retrospectively toward the 'essential kernel of rationality' that can be found in the Enlightenment and that would have to be preserved in any event; they will be oriented toward the 'contemporary limits of the necessary', that is, toward what is not or is no longer indispensable for the constitution of ourselves as autonomous subjects. (1984: 6)

This project becomes more important under today's human-centred assumptions, with the exhaustion and turning inwards of liberal framings of the subject. Foucault indicated that, with this shift, rather than the liberal subject emancipating itself through its growth and the transformation of its circumstances, there was no longer the starting assumption of a transformative subject driving progress and emancipation. There was still a focus on the subject, but this was a subject unable to know or to transform: thus, the human subject becomes the object of transformative practices of governance as development rather than the subject of development as external transformation.

The sphere of government action is that of governance: of enabling the subject to construct itself, to empower itself. In this process, power or government finally disappears, dissolving itself into society. Government is no longer conceived as wise management directing or controlling society as in the pre-modern age of Machiavelli, nor is government based on developing society and calculative progress as in the age of the classical liberalism of modernity, where mass society and the nation-state meant that 'society must be defended' (see Foucault 2003, 2007). With the decline of liberal conceptions of modernity, Foucault suggests that the liberal world is reduced to work on the governance of the self. Amartya Sen's capabilities approach to development fits squarely into this analysis. Sen critiques both the market-based liberal conception of the rational autonomous individual capable of assuming responsibility for its own development and also the state-based, top-down social democratic conception of the subject as passive and the object of social engineering projects of modernization. For Sen, the individual is the only agent of development, but the individual is constructed as a vulnerable subject needing the enabling of external agency: the individual is thereby both the ends and the means of 'development as freedom'.

Development after the colonial/post-colonial problematic

At the centre of the shift from development as material progress to development as inner progress is the problematization of the inner world of the subject. Rather than the assumption of *Homo œconomicus*, the rational decision-maker, there is an emphasis on the importance of differentiated subjectivity – on superstition, culture, ethics and irrationality – to decision-making. As Sen argues, there is no evidence for the view that individuals engage in rational choice-making on the basis of the pursuit of rational self-interest. In his view, the liberal understanding that 'we live in a world of reasonably well-informed people acting intelligently in pursuit of their self-interests' is misplaced as our intersubjective understandings and affectivities mean that it is the human subject itself which introduces difference and inequality into the analysis (1987: 17). Once there is no universal rational subject, but different rationalities, choice-making begins to open up as a sphere for understanding difference and for intervening on the basis of overcoming or ameliorating difference. As Sen notes:

> ... to attach importance to the agency aspect of each person does not entail accepting whatever a person happens to value as being valuable ... Respecting the agency aspect points to the appropriateness of going beyond a person's well-being into his or her valuations, commitments, etc. but the necessity of assessing these valuations ... is not eliminated ... [E]ven though 'the use of one's agency is, in an important sense, a matter for oneself to judge', the need for careful assessment of aims, objectives, allegiances, etc., and of the conception of the good, may be important and exacting. (Ibid.: 42)

The human-centred critique of liberal rationalist economic assumptions necessarily focuses on the inner life of the human subject. The understanding of irrational outcomes of market competition is transferred from the study of capitalist social relations to the study of irrational (non-universalist) human motivations and understandings. The crucial facet of this approach in economic theorizing, often called 'new institutionalism' (see, for example, North 1990, 2005), is that differences in outcomes can be understood as conscious, subjective choices, rather than as structurally imposed outcomes (as discussed in the previous chapter). The important research focus is then the individual making the choices and the subjectively created institutional frameworks (formal and informal) structuring these choices. This is a societal perspective which starts from the individual as a decision-maker and then works outwards to understand why 'wrong' choices are made, rather than equipping the individual with a set of universal rational capacities and understanding the differences in outcomes as products of social and economic contexts and relationships. This perspective is much more individual-focused, but the individual subject is understood in isolation from their social and economic relations. 'Wrong' choices are understood first in terms of institutional blockages at the level of custom, ideology and ideas and then in terms of the formal institutional blockages – the incentives and opportunities available to enable other choices. This problematization of the individual shares much with therapeutic approaches, which also work at the level of the individual (attempting to remove psychological blockages to making better choices) rather than at the level of social or economic relations.

As Foucault noted, the work of these agent-centred, new-institutionalist theorists was not narrowly concerned with economic theory; the institutionalist approach was closely tied to psychological and sociological framings and drew on legal and historical problematics, raising 'a whole series of problems that are more historical and institutional than specifically economic, but which opened the way for very interesting research on the political-institutional framework of the development of capitalism, and from which the American neo-liberals benefited' (2008: 135). Of particular importance, for this chapter, is the impact of these ideas on United Nations development programmes and World Bank policy-making frameworks in the 1990s, which can be clearly traced in the influence of writers such as Douglass North and, of course, Amartya Sen.

I want to suggest that while new institutionalist approaches became dominant only after the end of the Cold War, their appearance, especially in the field of international relations, can be genealogically traced through the discourse of development as a defensive understanding of the gap between the promise of freedom and economic progress under the universalist teleological framing of liberal modernity and the limits to this telos in the lack of economic, social and political progress and the failure to generalize liberal modes of government in the colonial and post-colonial world.

Colonialism was substantially politically challenged and put on the defensive only with the First World War, which led to the rise of the discourses of universal rights of self-determination, articulated both by Lenin, with the birth of the revolutionary Soviet Union, and by US president Woodrow Wilson, with America's rise to world power and aspiration to weaken the European colonial powers. Once brought into the universalist liberal framework of understanding, the discourse of development was used to both legitimize and to negotiate the gradual withdrawal of colonial power. Given its clearest intellectual articulation in Lord Lugard's *Dual Mandate* (1923), British colonial domination was justified on the basis that the difference between the Western subject and the colonial subject was a question of culture and values – a problem of the inner world of the subject – preventing the colonial subject from transforming the external world, from economic and social development. Lugard was the first to articulate an institutionalist understanding of development, concerned as much with the inculcation of values and understanding through the export of political institutions of integration, as with economic progress itself. Development was conceived as the barrier to self-determination, as much as the achievement of development was conceived as a justification for external rule, for it was through Western 'enlightened' knowledge and experience of transforming the external world that the colonial subject could be emancipated.

The discourse of development, of the 'dual mandate', of serving both British imperial interests and the self-interest of the colonial subject, could be construed as a discourse of 'development as freedom', but one very different to that articulated three-quarters of a century later by Sen. For the colonial mind, the cultural and moral incapacities of the colonial subject prevented development, and therefore it was a civilizational task of transforming the subject to create the conditions for autonomy, for the emergence of the liberal subject – for freedom as self-determination. In Lugard's own words:

> As Roman imperialism laid the foundation of modern civilisation, and led the wild barbarians of these islands [Britain] along the path of progress, so in Africa today we are repaying the debt and bringing to the dark places of the earth, the abode of barbarism and cruelty, the torch of culture and progress ... If there is unrest, and a desire for independence, as in India and Egypt, it is because we have taught the values of liberty and freedom ... Their very discontent is a measure of their progress. (Ibid.: 618)

As Foucault notes in his reflections upon Kant's *What is Enlightenment?*, the Enlightenment project of civilizing those not enlightened enough to civilize themselves was seen to be the work of external agency. In order to be freed, the subject first had to be subjected – just as the civilized Romans had to subject the barbarian Britons. Of course, it was not surprising that the denial of liberal universalist understandings of the subject – explicit in colonial rule and the denial of formal liberal freedoms of self-rule and sovereign independence – should take a civilizational focus. Social and economic difference was used to justify the denial of political and legal equality and at the same time subordinated to universality through the assumption that the colonial power was capable of assisting the colonial subject in its journey towards 'development', understood as a higher and more enlightened, 'modern' or 'liberal' existence.

The discourse of development can, of course, be critically engaged with in the manner of Edward Said's Foucault-inspired, ground-breaking framework of *Orientalism* (1995), as presupposing 'Western superiority and Oriental inferiority' (ibid.: 42). There can be little doubt that the birth of the Enlightenment brought with it a Euro-centric view of the world that was universalistic in its assumptions that differences would be progressively overcome through 'development' (see also Wolff 1994; Todorova 1997; Burgess 1997). This understanding of progress as a universal teleology, demarcating those states and societies which were more and less 'advanced', was based on the presupposition that the Enlightenment brought economic and social progress to the West and demonstrated a path which could be universally replicated through the enlightenment of the colonial subject.

However, what is missing in this framework is the distinct difference between the discourse of development under colonialism (and in much of the early post-colonial era) and the understanding of development under today's agent-centred assumptions. The colonial subject was not seen as a liberal subject, but a subject understood as lacking autonomy – the liberal subject had to be created in the case of the colonial 'exception', on the assumption that the subject could become a liberal and thereby an autonomous and self-governing subject. Here 'development' was separated temporally and spatially from 'freedom'. In the classical liberal modernist teleology, the liberal world would expand spatially as the external world progressed temporally towards 'freedom'. There was a liberal teleology of progress, which was expressed in both spatial and temporal terms; in terms of a liberal 'inside' and a non-liberal 'outside', seen as shrinking with the progress of development. Development was the mechanism through which the world would be universalized, through which the gap between the liberal vision of the future and the realities of the present would be bridged.

The discourse of 'the West and the Rest' (Hall 2007), of the liberal and the colonial/post-colonial world, articulated the limits of liberalism as external, thereby giving an ontological content to development in terms of both spatiality and temporality. There could only be discourses of spatial and temporal differentiation with the understanding that the limits to liberal universalist frameworks of understanding were external ones. The key point to understand with regard to today's articulation of 'development as freedom' is that the bifurcation – both in spatial and temporal terms – between the West and the Rest has been overcome through a universalizing framework which internalizes rather than externalizes the limits of liberalism. Once limits are internalized, development inverts the relationship between freedom and necessity. As discussed in Chapter 2, without a spatial and temporal conception of external structures, freedom becomes the problem rather than necessity.

The internalizing of the understanding of limits, alleged to be a condition of our globalized and interconnected world, starts from the basis that we are all liberal autonomous, self-determining subjects – that we are free in a liberal sense, but that we are not 'free' in human-centred terms, i.e. that liberal 'freedoms' are no longer adequate or central to 'freedom'. In this framing, differences are internally generated: through the fact that individuals make decisions and choices in complex, embedded and often irrational ways. Rather than the lack of 'will' – of subjective choice-making capacity – being the exception, explaining the contingent nature of spatial and temporal limits to universalizing progress, the differentiated nature of individual or communal capacity is the norm, explaining the inevitable existence of difference and inequality. Here we have a very different universalism, one which universalizes the understanding of the vulnerable subject, in need of development understood in terms of adaptive capacities. In this respect, development becomes a permanent project of self-development, of freeing the subject from its inner limitations. This project is necessarily inclusive because there is no longer any 'outside'.

Sen's framework

In Amartya Sen's 'agent-centred' world there are no external universals and therefore there is no framework or yardstick for an external measurement of development. The transformative project of development is reduced down to that of enlarging individual agency understood as the choice-making capacity of the subject able to adapt to external necessity. Freedom now becomes an internal process of empowerment, one with no fixed measure of comparison and no fixed end or goal (the embrace of necessity presupposes no goal outside the individual). Where the colonial subject needed development for the fixed and universal goal of self-government as freedom, Sen's subject is involved in an ongoing struggle for 'freedom' in which the inner life of the individual is both the means for freedom and the measure of freedom:

> Expansion of freedom is viewed, in this approach, both as the primary end and as the principal means of development. Development consists in the removal of various types of unfreedoms that leave people with little choice and little opportunity of exercising their reasoned agency. (1999: xii)

Individuals have to be freed from 'unfreedoms', which can take both material and immaterial or ideological forms. Freedom here is not articulated in a classical liberal framing of the constitution of an autonomous subject. Where Sen goes beyond the framings of liberal modernity is that development and freedom can only be understood in relation to the inner world of the individual.

Development, understood in terms of adaptive capacities, cannot be measured materially because these capacities are internal to the individual (or internal to the society or community which is the object of our human-centred concern). Capabilities cannot be measured in terms of surface outcomes: a society may be healthy or wealthy but still lack adaptive capabilities. This is because wealth may have stemmed from good fortune or specific characteristics, which cannot be sustained or cannot be replicated. The capabilities approach is not directly concerned with the material outcomes of development policies, nor is it directly concerned with the inputs provided to individuals. At the heart of the concern with adaptive capacity is the inner capability of individuals to choose 'freely' what is in their own and their society's interests. It is the lifestyle choices, freely made, which count. As Martha Nussbaum stresses: 'There is a huge moral difference between a policy that promotes health and one that promotes health capabilities – the latter, not the former, honors the person's lifestyle choices' (2011: 26). The inculcation of adaptive capabilities is hostile to functionalist or utilitarian approaches, which would support paternalistic or coercive health interventions for societal ends.[3] It is the process of individual choice-making which counts, not the social outcome; both Sen and Nussbaum ascribe a high value to choice, and place it at the centre of their moral philosophical frameworks (see ibid.).

The central point I wish to make here is not that development is degraded to a subjective level of the material resources which are considered necessary or desirable for the sustainability of poverty, maintaining the 'bare life' of the 'uninsured' (Duffield 2007), but that the subject and object of development – understood as capability- or capacity-building – is entirely internalized. Development is judged on the basis of the individual's use of 'reasoned agency'. Development is the project of giving the individual the choice-making capacity necessary to adapt efficiently – to become resilient – in today's globalized world. Development is the task of all stakeholders but can be measured only in the individual's inner achievement of 'freedom'. Freedom thereby cannot be conceptualized in the liberal terminology of autonomy, self-government or democracy. Here, freedom is a continuum, the goal of which is never reached as barriers or 'unfreedoms' to 'reasoned agency' can always reappear and can only be known post hoc. This is why Sen talks of the 'expansion of freedom', never of the achievement of freedom.

The individual's 'freedom' is conceptually crucial for Sen and becomes the starting point, the means and the end point for understanding human development in terms of capabilities:

> Societal arrangements, involving many institutions (the state, the market, the legal system, political parties, the media, public interest groups and public discussion forums, among others), are investigated in terms of their contribution to enhancing and guaranteeing the substantive freedoms of individuals, seen as active agents of change, rather than as passive recipients of dispensed benefits. (1999: xii–xiii)

If people are not exercising 'reasoned choice-making' then there is something wrong with the institutions of society and the inner world of opinions and beliefs. If choice-making is limited or unreasoned then people lack freedom, and development is necessary to act on the institutions which are blocking this process of free and reasoned choice-making. Unlike liberal framings, in which the interests of the subject are revealed through their preferences and choices, here choices are understood as '*adaptive*' products of individuals' lack of freedom, like the fox in the fable who calls the grapes sour after he finds that he cannot reach them (Nussbaum 2011: 54). Governments are understood to be responsible for enabling the development of this reasoning capacity, not for the material provision of life's necessities to enable freedom as an assumed capacity for choice-making. In liberal discourse, the provision of food and nutrition to the poor would be seen as a valuable step to enabling free choice-making; however, in the agent-centred discourse of adaptive capacities, the provision of food is no more an answer to famine than it is to lack of nutrition, as 'a policy that just doles out food to people rather than giving them choice in matters of nutrition is insufficiently respectful of their freedom' (ibid.: 56).

We begin to see here that Sen's framework is doing a lot more than merely downplaying the need for material development or taking the social struggle out of the process of freeing individuals from oppression. Sen's framing of development, in terms of the inculcation of individual capabilities, takes the understanding of socio-economic and political processes out of the framing of liberal modernity. There is no teleology of progress as an external measure of growth in human well-being, there is no universalist framing and there is no longer the understanding of the liberal subject – as either a rights- or an interest-bearing rational and autonomous actor.

For the capabilities approach to adaptive capacity, there is no such thing as the universal liberal subject, there are merely capacity differentials in choice-making which are constituted through the 'unfreedoms' with which individuals are confronted. Here the subject is autonomous but not 'free'. The subject is autonomous as a choice-making actor, but never truly capable of making a 'free and reasoned' choice. Freedom – choice-making capacity – has always to be expanded. This need for the expansion of freedom is as necessary for Western subjects as for post-colonial subjects. For Sen, there is no divide between the West and the Rest, no sphere of liberalism and sphere of non-liberalism or aliberalism. This is as inclusive an analysis as can be imagined, and in this way evades or bypasses the immanent contradiction between the Enlightenment's metaphysical conception of the rational, transformative universal subject and the limits posed by the social relations of capitalist modernity. The contradictions of liberalism are not overcome externally – through the transformation of social relations – but shifted to a different sphere of intelligibility, through understanding material difference as a product of the choice-making individual – universalized precisely upon the basis of the differentiation of individuals as irreducible choice-making subjects.

Sen, in his work, uses this view of the differentiated subject as irreducible agent to evade or efface all liberal binaries based on the construction of legal or political collectivities. The starting point of the freedom of individual agency is at the centre of all his wide-ranging studies: whether it is deconstructing the idea of material equality (judged by an external measure of equal opportunities or resources or of equal outcomes) (Sen 1992); deconstructing the idea of collective identities (Sen 2006); deconstructing ideas of justice (on the basis that formal frameworks of politics and law cannot measure how individuals grow as choice-makers) (Sen 2009); or deconstructing material measures of development (Sen 1999). For Sen, there is no divide between the West and the non-West as there are no exclusive social or economic collectivities – the level of development in terms of GDP is no longer of decisive relevance, nor is the type of political regime in itself. There is no universal external yardstick available to give content to freedom in either the economic and social or the political and legal realms. The lack of freedom can exist as much in a wealthy liberal democracy as under any other society, as the concern is not with an 'exclusionary' liberal modernist understanding of freedom. Any individual can become unfree if Sen's conception of 'the more inclusive idea of capability deprivation' is taken up (ibid.: 20).

In this conception, political freedom and market economic competition are to be valued because they help facilitate individual choice-making capacities, thereby enabling efficient adaption to changing circumstances. The assumption is that without 'development' individuals will not be free, in the sense that they will lack the capabilities necessary to pursue their reasoned goals. Here none of us is free from the need for development. Development is the process of altering the institutions that shape our capacities and capabilities for free choices. In this understanding of freedom, there can be no assumption of originatory or universal autonomy and rationality, such as that underpinning social contract theorizing: the mainstay of the political and legal subject of liberal modernity. To this *'arrangement-focused'* view, Sen counter-posits a *'realization-focused* understanding of justice' (2009: 10). For Sen, justice, like development, cannot be universal but understood only in terms of individual empowerment and capacity-building.

> The question to ask, then, is this, if the justice of what happens in a society depends on a combination of institutional features and actual behavioural characteristics, along with other influences that determine the social realizations, then is it possible to identify 'just' institutions for a society without making them contingent on actual behaviour[?] ... Indeed, we have good reason for recognizing that the pursuit of *justice is partly a matter of the gradual formation of behaviour patterns* ... (Ibid.: 68, emphasis added)

Justice is not a matter of liberal institutional arrangements but about empowering or capability-building individuals; there is no abstract universalism but rather the recognition that 'realization' comes first. On the basis of injustice, or 'unfreedoms', then justice (like development) becomes a process of realization 'aimed at guiding social choice towards social justice' (ibid.: 69). Justice aims at enlarging justice as freedom in the same way as development aims at enlarging development as freedom. Justice is a continuous process, not a fixed and externally measurable end or goal.

Sen's displacement of the external world with the inner world

For Sen, there are no universal external frames of reference. It is not liberal institutions or economic development which serve to gauge the problematic of the subject but the 'realization of the individual's capabilities' – this as an ongoing process, not a measurement against a fixed point. Sen, in his work on *Justice*, is keen to highlight the importance of difference over universality – the embeddedness of the human subject. In doing so, he quotes Gramsci:

> In acquiring one's conception of the world one always belongs to a particular grouping which is that of all the social elements which share the same mode of thinking and acting. We are all conformists of some conformism or other, always man-in-the-mass or collective man. (Ibid.: 119)

Sen suggests here that it is our social embeddedness which restricts our capacities for transition. We need an 'anthropological way' (ibid.: 120, 121) of understanding how our subjectivities may constitute a barrier to the development of public reason. He expands on how our 'local conventions of thought' (ibid.: 125) may limit our ability to adapt and become resilient subjects; that individual and collective understandings may be partial and one-sided. However, this is not just a call for more information or greater material equality. The key to Sen's perspective of development as freedom is capabilities. It is not instrumental outcomes per se, nor resource inputs, but the individual's 'capability to choose' (ibid.: 235).

It is vital to draw out that 'capability to choose' is very different from the 'freedom to choose'. The latter conception is that of classical liberalism, which assumes that freedom is all that is required for the rational autonomous subject. The former is the key to understanding Sen's human- or agent-centred perspective. Sen disagrees with the liberal perspective, which assumes autonomy is freedom. For Sen, freedom is an ongoing process of empowering the individual; this empowerment is not measured in external outputs but internal processes of valuation and decision-making. It is not an outcome, not even a non-material outcome, such as 'well-being' or 'happiness' (ibid.: 271). It is an internal outcome – it is a 'way of living' (ibid.: 273).

Sen's work, in fact, recaptures some of the elitist theorizing of Plato in focusing on the inner world rather than the outer world. Sen, in a footnote, states (ibid.: 301):

> In seeing freedom in terms of the power to bring about the outcome one wants with reasoned assessment, there is, of course, the underlying question whether the person has had an adequate opportunity to reason about what she really wants. Indeed the opportunity of *reasoned assessment* cannot but be an important part of any substantive understanding of freedom.

Sen is essentially seeking to measure the internal or moral life of the subject and arguing that this should be the actual object of policy-making and also the indirect means of measuring the extent of 'freedom'. The internal capacities of individuals are revealed only in relation to the choices which they make, in their own understandings of their own needs and interests. Subjects which lack the adaptive capacities for resilience therefore are held to choose poorly, to reveal not their potential efficient adaptive capacities but merely their lack of 'freedom'. Martha Nussbaum stresses the distinction between this agent-centred assumption, that interests are not revealed in subject choices, and the liberal rationalist assumption that the subject is only a subject because they are rational choice-makers:

> the Capabilities Approach is not based upon subjective preferences, although it takes preferences seriously. It argues strongly against preference-based approaches within development economics and within philosophy. It views preferences as often unreliable for political purposes. Only the most fully corrected informed-desire approaches play even a subsidiary role in political justification. (Nussbaum 2011: 80)

This very much follows the pre-liberal framing of Plato in *Gorgias*, when Socrates famously argued with Polus that tyrants lacked power because they lacked a true understanding of their ends, of what would do them good (Plato 1960: 35–9). In other words, the subjects of development are not able to autonomously or rationally judge what is in their own interests in terms of the adaptive choices necessary for a fully resilient society. For Sen, the subject in need of development is one who lacks the capacity to answer the Socratic question: 'How should one live?' (Sen 1987: 2). For Sen, development – the task of good governance – is necessary to enable individuals to answer this question correctly, in terms of the active embrace of necessity. In fact, Sen turns back on Plato his assumption that there is no such thing as evil, merely ignorance, suggesting with regard to the parochial understanding of the Greeks, in their practice of infanticide, that even Plato suffered from a limited and narrow 'local' understanding of the world (2009: 404–7). People choosing to live badly – the limits of human reason – constitute the demand for and limit of governance: of 'development as freedom'.

Where does this leave the human subject in Sen? On one level the human subject is all that there is. The goal of policy-making is the enabling and the empowering of this subject – of fulfilling its capabilities and capacities. But the human subject does not set goals; the human subject has no agency and no measuring capacity itself. The human subject is the end to be achieved, through the process of development, justice, democracy, etc. – the project of humanizing is the human. For Sen, as for Plato, the project is an internal one rather than an external one. As Foucault suggests, this focus on the inner life connects Platonic thought with Christian thought, similarly denying transformative agency upon the external world (2010: 359).

This shift to work on the inner self rather than the external world enables us to understand development as a process of freedom. As Martha Nussbaum argues, governments need to pay specific attention to the fluid and dynamic nature of an individual's *internal capabilities*, which can be best enhanced through education and physical and emotional health and support (2011: 21). Those who most need to be 'freed' are the poor and marginal who need 'enabling': those who lack the means to adapt; those who are vulnerable need to be empowered, capability-built and secured through resilience (WRI 2008). Wherever there is a decision to be made, this provides the interventionist nexus for 'development'. The discourse of external necessity imposes itself through the interrogations of agent-centred governance: 'How can this decision or this choice be better made?' 'How can the institutions of governance help enable a better "choice environment"?' 'What capabilities do the poor and marginalized need to enable this choice?'

The human-centred logic, so well articulated by Sen, sets out a framework of understanding and of policy-making which focuses on the internal life of individuals as shaped by the immediate context of family and child-rearing, especially the transition to the decision-making subject. The 2007 *World Development Report, Development and the Next Generation*, provides a good example of this approach:

> Decisions during the five youth transitions have the biggest long-term impacts on how human capital is kept safe, developed, and deployed: continuing to learn, starting to work, developing a family, and exercising citizenship … Young people and their families make the decisions – but policies and institutions also affect the risks, the opportunities, and ultimately the outcomes. (World Bank 2006: 2)

Development as freedom means capability-building starts often with the young as a way of transforming society through reshaping their internal worlds.[4] The report's discussion of how decision-making can be altered is quoted below:

> If death rates are the benchmark, young people are a healthy group: the average 10 year-old has a 97 percent chance to reach the age of 25. Mortality is a misleading measure of youth health, however, because it does not reflect the behaviour that puts their health at risk later on. Youth is when people begin smoking, consuming

alcohol and drugs, engaging in sex, and having more control over their diet and physical activity – behaviours that persist and affect their future health …

Because the (sometimes catastrophic) health consequences of these behaviours show up only later in life, they are much more difficult and expensive to treat than to prevent. But for many young people, the search for a stable identity, combined with short time horizons and limited information, encourages them to experiment with activities that put their health at risk … Reducing risk-taking among youth requires that they have the information and the capacity to make and act on decisions. Policies can do much to help young people manage these risks, especially if they make young people more aware of the long-term consequences of their actions today … (ibid.: 8)

The logic of the argument is that social and economic problems are the result of poor choice-making, especially by young people. Development no longer takes the form of economic and social transformation but of capability-building: empowering the poor and marginal to make better choices and thereby to become more resilient to external threats and pressures. In the deterministic approach of human-centred understandings, capability- and capacity-building can never start early enough, if every individual is to be fully empowered. As Martha Nussbaum argues:

Empirical studies show that early intervention is crucial, building the case for pre-school interventions and programs that partner with families … a great deal of human potential is being wasted by a failure to intervene early, both through programs designed to enhance future human beings' health *in utero* and through programmes after birth. (2011: 194)

Once the focus upon human development is on the internal capacities of the individual, the understanding of problems of conflict or of a lack of development involves a retreat into the internal world of the human mind. According to Nussbaum, the development of '*basic capabilities*' is not a product of nature, not 'hardwired in the DNA', but rather is a product of human intervention and therefore it is for government policy-making to ensure the correct 'maternal nutrition and prenatal experience' (ibid.: 23). Once the problem is no longer the material circumstances, but the subject's lack of freedom – their lack of capability to respond efficiently to their circumstances – the agent-centred discourse of capacity-building tends to infantalize those subject to development interventions.

This infantalization is clearly illustrated by Nussbaum, who argues that the capabilities approach can be applied to non-human animals as much as to humans. Once the rational capacity for choice-making is denied to the human political subject – as it necessarily is in all human-centred approaches which argue that the political subject has to be constructed through government intervention in societal processes – then there is no basis for liberal representative political and legal theory. Subject-centred governance practices cannot derive their legitimacy through representational theory that assumes universal rationality, such as contract theory, which assumes representational equality. Nussbaum, for example, explicitly argues that animals and other sentient beings with agency can be considered to be 'subjects of a political theory of justice, whether or not they are capable of understanding or assessing that theory' (ibid.: 88; 157–63). The discourses of human development and of capacity- and capability-building, in assuming that the human subject is the source of problems of conflict and underdevelopment, inevitably end up reducing the status of the subject (as can been seen in the post-human framings, articulated by Cudworth and Hobden 2011; and in the rise of new materialist or object-based theorizing – see, for example, Bennett 2010a; Harman 2010). The internal gaze of human-centred discourse ends up removing the subject itself, not merely the importance of the material relations of its external world.

Conclusion

The human subject may be at the centre of development discourse, but it is this subject's lack of capability which is highlighted. This human-centred approach replicates that of Kant's idealist or voluntarist understanding of the internal and individual nature of barriers to enlightenment. The lack of material development is read as evidence of the lack of the subject's capabilities to efficiently adapt and to actively embrace necessity. In a globalized world, with access to information and resources, it appears that the subject of development is exercising agency in choosing poorly and, in effect, is the object of its own subjection and lack of self-realization. The subject's difference or otherness is understood and confirmed by its constructed world of economic and social inequalities. The fact that we accept the universal understanding of the autonomous choice-making subject now becomes an apologia for difference rather than a call for its transcendence. The source of this difference is then located in the subject itself, in the inner world of the subject. The problems of development or the barriers to the eradication of difference are then searched for in terms of the difficulty of changing the cognitive frameworks of the subject. As will be considered further in the following two chapters, on the social construction of difference and the shifting understandings of intervention, the understanding of barriers to progress as internal rather than external results in the growing acceptance of inequalities as inevitable or as a product of choice and the proliferation of external regimes of interference and regulation.

5 | THE SOCIAL CONSTRUCTION OF DIFFERENCE

Introduction

As we have seen in the previous chapters, human-centred discourses remove the social mediation of the world. The world is the one we produce through our own agency and therefore the one that we bear responsibility for. However, the lack of social mediation means that there is no shared world that we can all relate to; in effect we all create our own multiple worlds which to some extent may be overlapping, depending on the question of concern and the level of analysis. We are held to create our world as individuals, bearing responsibility for our lifestyle choices, but also presumed to create our world as families or communities, which are often seen to have generated or reinforced environmental or societal problems such as poor parenting or crime. We are also held responsible for the creation of our world at the level of states, with problematic national cultures or state–society relations, and we are told we create the world at the global level, when we face the problems of man-made global warming or the global financial crisis.

In the human-centred world, in which necessity increasingly appears to assert itself over human freedom, our understanding of the world begins to lose any sense of meaningful structures of contingency. As we saw in the previous chapter, the less mediation there is perceived to be between our actions and decisions and their outcomes, the more the world loses its material qualities. Once the structures of material social relations disappear from our analysis, it appears that human freedom – or at least actions and choices – constructs the world as it appears. The removal of external or 'blind' necessity as the field through which human freedom can be constituted, through the understanding and transformation of economic and social processes, reduces human choice-making to work on the self in adaption to the external world. If we focus on the human – as problematic actor and choice-maker – we tend to explain the differences and inequalities in wealth and social power, which are all too apparent in the world, on the basis of the behavioural choices made by people themselves (either collectively or individually).

The agent-centred approach understands human action and choice-making as primary – as constitutive of the world of appearances. It is from these appearances that we are then alleged to be able to work backwards to find the source of human causation. The increasing dominance of necessity over freedom can be clearly seen in the shifting frameworks in which change has been understood in the international sphere. This chapter charts the problematization of agency and the construction of problems in terms of vulnerable subjects and analyses how this shift has been reflected in our understandings of the barriers to change, through three conceptually distinct and chronologically distinguishable stages: the early-1990s view that liberal transformation would be universalized with the Cold War victory of liberal ideals and the spread of new global norms of good governance; the mid- to late-1990s view that barriers to the promotion of social and economic transformation could be understood as the product of state or elite self-interests; and the agent-centred perspective, dominant since the 2000s, that the promotion of security and development necessarily involves much deeper and more extensive external intervention in order to 'free' the subject through first transforming social institutions and societal practices. Through charting the shifts in the understanding of international norms of governance, this chapter seeks to highlight the problems inherent in human-centred discourses that emphasize the importance of subjective agency, normative choices and cultural and ideational frameworks of understanding.

A key problem which will be emphasized is that in the downplaying of social and economic context, agency-based understandings tend to degrade the rational capacities of – and to exoticize and problematize – the subjects of human-centred policy interventions. The social constructivist approach, which presupposes a closed or endogenous framework of societal reproduction, has thereby been a crucial paradigm through which discursive representations have shifted to emphasizing the subjective policy barrier posed by the alleged 'vulnerabilities' implicit in the mind-sets of those subject to human-centred capacity-building interventions. Vulnerabilities are defined as the barriers to becoming a resilient subject. In this sense vulnerabilities constitute our 'unfreedoms' or the restrictions, both material and ideological, which prevent us from embracing necessity. The barriers to adaptation constitute vulnerabilities, and subjects which lack the capabilities necessary to become resilient are therefore constructed as vulnerable. This characterization as vulnerable can be applied to individuals – the 'at risk', 'socially excluded' or the 'marginal' – as well as to communities – the 'poor', 'indigenous' or the 'environmentally threatened' – as much as to states themselves – the 'failing', 'failed', 'fragile', 'low income under stress' or badly governed. This chapter examines the interventionist discourses of the international sphere which seek to overcome the vulnerabilities of post-colonial and post-conflict states and communities through the inculcation of resilience understood as behaviour modification.

The construction of problems in the international sphere as products of subjects, understood to be vulnerable and therefore to be potentially dangerous (both to themselves and to others), has become a core theme of human-centred discourses. However, it should be noted that this framework which exoticizes and problematizes the human subject is a universal one: the gaze of agent-centred understandings constructs problems in terms of the actions of vulnerable subjects. In this way, domestic problems are often constructed through the problematization of those who are characterized as bad parents, criminals, the unemployed, the obese, smokers, etc. The human-centred characterization of vulnerable subjects as constitutive of the social, economic or environmental problems being addressed by governance interventions that aim to inculcate resilience has already been touched upon, in the analysis of discourses of societal resilience and development as capacity-building. As will be seen below, the discourses of resilience and capacity-building are entirely imbricated within those of vulnerability, where it is understood that appeals to reason – for example, through health information or public engagement – can no longer be effective if people lack the capacity to govern themselves according to 'adaptive', 'civic' or 'other-regarding' reason.

The discursive construction of agent-centred worlds, at the heart of the human-centred problematic, dissolves the external world as an object which potentially brings us together. Seeking to address problems from the starting point of the individual agent, or the human mind, produces a world which appears highly differentiated. The internalized understandings of agent-centred approaches then operate to frame this differentiated world as a product of distinct and overlapping endogenous processes, which can apparently explain the differences and inequalities in the world of appearances. The construction of a segmented and differentiated world may seem to be a far cry from the assumptions of global civil society and constructions of the world as a 'global neighbourhood' in the 1990s (CGG 1995). However, by focusing on the role of sociological institutionalism or social constructivism in the understanding of agency and societal change since the early 1990s, this chapter will highlight how the vulnerable subject has moved to the centre of our explanations of the problems of the international sphere.

Promoting reason

At the end of the Cold War, the resolution of problems of the international sphere – problems both of conflict and of international economic inequalities – became increasingly conceptualized in terms of the international diffusion of global liberal norms, of human rights, the rule of law and good governance (see, for example, McFaul 2004; Carothers 2004; Youngs 2002; Thomas 2011). Norms are generally understood as shared meanings or expectations with regard to the standards of appropriate behaviour.[1] The study of global norms and their diffusion entered the mainstream of international relations (IR) theory with the constructivist understanding that state interests and identities were heavily influenced through intersubjective engagement within the international sphere itself. From the early 1990s onwards, it was argued that as the world became more globalized, states increasingly shared the standards of behaviour ascribed to progressive liberal norms (Finnemore 1996a).

In the academic discourses of the 1990s, theoretical work on the diffusion of liberal norms was understood to be successfully challenging and overcoming the realist framings of the international sphere. The classical liberal, or rationalist, framework of subjects as atomized, autonomous self-interested actors[2] was dominant in the discipline of international relations during the Cold War period, where it was understood that states entered the international arena with preformed interests which they then rationally or strategically pursued in the international sphere. Constructivist, agent-centred theorists inverted this understanding of the international sphere, asserting that states' understandings of their own interests and identities were socially – intersubjectively – constructed: that states co-constituted themselves and the international sphere through their collective interaction (Wendt 1992). Exogenous factors and relations were removed – the structuring of the international sphere was the product of states' own intersubjective choices and interactions. This framing freed states from the external structural constraints of realism, allowing a much more agent-centred understanding, in which ideational factors, rather than material constraints, played a major role in the understanding of international change. Within this context, work on liberal norms and their diffusion became an important area of international academic and policy concern (for a good overview, see Cortell and Davis 2000).

This chapter first sets up the development of sociological agent-based theorizing in international relations and then draws out how this discourse of liberal norm promotion became the basis of an agent-centred understanding of the limits to progress. Agent-based approaches to understanding the international sphere will, for analytical purposes, be broken down into three broad stages:[3] 'first generation', late-1980s to mid-1990s understandings, which highlighted the social construction of shared meanings in the international sphere; 'second generation' agency-based approaches, in the mid- to late 1990s, which emphasized the barriers of state elites and the role of non-state-based actors, in the extension and diffusion of global liberal norms; and, in the 2000s, 'third generation', human-centred approaches, which stressed the importance of differential and distinct domestic ideational frameworks, with an emphasis on the cultural embeddedness of the vulnerable subject. For this 'third generation' of norm-theorizing, the global sphere is a striated and differentiated one, where liberal norm diffusion needs to be understood as a much more contingent and problematic project.

Sociological, agency-based approaches have thus shifted focus from the closed framing of intersubjective engagement in the international sphere, in which actors were understood to be collectively self-constituting – freed from the structural constraints of exogenous interests – to the frameworks of ideational reproduction within states and societies held to be resistant to liberal norms. This chapter highlights the way in which human-centred understandings have become dominant in international relations through the development and application of endogenous agency-based approaches to the international sphere and the transfer of their application to the domestic level of the vulnerable or 'failing' state. Whereas the focus on culture, norms and identity could perhaps have been understood to be innovative for international relations theorizing, the transfer of this methodological approach to the problems faced by many post-conflict or post-colonial states has facilitated the exoticization and problematization of these states and their populations as vulnerable. In this way, human-centred approaches reproduce and give new life to previously discredited endogenous frameworks of understanding, which have historically been used to rationalize gross inequalities of treatment on the basis of apparently inherent cultural and societal distinctions.

In removing exogenous structural or material constraints, the constructivist gaze understands problems of conflict or social and economic inequality through the reproduction of ideational choices, rather than as reflecting material economic or socio-political structural constraints (Checkel 1998; see also Hay 2006; Peters 2005: 107–22; Scott 2008). These choices are then either to be accepted and possibly celebrated or supported as political resistances to liberal norms (see, for example, Richmond 2010) or, more often, seen as problematic cultural and ideational barriers which necessitate much more intrusive modes of intervention in order to 'free' vulnerable populations held to lack the capacity to choose liberal norms for themselves.[4] This understanding of the barriers to the promotion of liberal norms, in increasingly ideational terms, shrinks the liberal world view: either celebrating perceived limits and resistances, thereby implicitly accepting material and structural inequalities as positive choices, or condemning social and cultural norms as moral and rational failings. Both of these framings 'exoticize' those subjects confronting societal inequalities and, in their exaggeration of difference, either operate as an apologia for existing social relations and inequalities or as the rationale for external projects of social engineering in order to 'civilize' or 'free' societies from their allegedly self-imposed ignorance and backwardness.

Social constructivism

In the wake of the unexpected collapse of the Soviet Union, agency-based, ideational approaches were advanced as a counter to earlier rationalist and structural materialist perspectives, which were now held to be unable to theorize transformational change (see, for example, Barnett 2008; Jackson and Sorensen 2010: 159–80; Reus-Smit 2001). The sociological perspective sought to demonstrate that states did not enter the international sphere with fixed identities and interests, but rather that their attitudes to political mechanisms of rule, including democratic institutions, were shaped and constructed through intersubjective engagement in the international sphere (see Wendt 1992, 1999). This framework both built on and challenged Cold War understandings of the extension of democratic norms and rights protections as a reflection of shared, preformed, rational economic interests (Katzenstein 1996b: 528). Where international relations theorists analysed shared normative understandings or the role of institutions in shaping behaviour, they tended to treat agreements on shared democratic norms (such as those emerging from the Helsinki process of the Organisation for Security and Co-operation, the Council of Europe or the European Commission) merely as external constraints to action (see, for example, Keohane 1989; Krasner 1983).

Neoliberal theorists[5] took a rationalist perspective to the study of international regimes and institutions, which were thereby understood to develop as part of the pursuit of existing self-interest: as minimizing transaction costs, facilitating the spread of information and overcoming uncertainties of international cooperation. In which case, the agency of actors could be understood merely as the reflection of their interests, held to be exogenous to their interaction in the international sphere. Constructivist approaches built upon this earlier work through challenging its underlying rationalist approach, and so freed the operation and development of agential choice from its material ties to preformed, exogenous subject interests:

> Neoliberal institutionalists explicitly acknowledge the collective rules (norms) that constrain and enable individual choice, but they continue to treat actor identities and interests themselves as preexisting and fixed. And to the extent that they *are* considered, norms (embodied in institutions) derive exclusively from rational egoistic choice. Their origins are thus limited to the preexisting preferences of agents, and their consequences tend to reflect this constraint. Identity thus remains marginalized, even in the more expansive neoliberal institutionalist arguments. (Kowert and Legro 1996: 458–9; see also Katzenstein 1996a: 11–17)

Social constructivism, by contrast, sought to emphasize the social environment in which states interacted and through which they constructed their self-identities and their perceptions of policy and governance needs (Katzenstein 1996a: 4). The emphasis on the international social context rather than exogenous social and political relations imposed a different understanding of the choices states as agents made in terms of liberal norms: one that emphasized the importance of global or international 'norms, identity and culture'.

Through working backwards, by process-tracing, theorists sought to establish how norms had both 'constitutive effects' in the inter-subjective construction of actor identities and 'regulative' effects describing 'collective expectations for proper behaviour', including domestic behaviour (ibid.: 5; see also Giddens 1984; Berger and Luckmann 1979). This framework emphasized the importance of transformative agency and ideas at the international level: reflecting upon 'how structures of constructed meaning, embodied in norms or identities, affect what states do' (Jepperson et al. 1996: 66). As Martha Finnemore put it:

> A constructivist approach does not deny that power and interest are important. They are. Rather, it asks a different and prior set of questions: it asks what interests *are*, and it investigates the ends to which and the means by which power will be used. The answers to these questions are not simply idiosyncratic and unique to each actor. The social nature of international politics creates normative understandings among actors that, in turn, coordinate values, expectations, and behaviour. (Finnemore 1996b: 157)

The two crucial grounding assumptions for this 'first generation' of agent-based norms theorizing were: first, that there was an increasingly global social environment influencing states' attitudes towards democratic norms; and, secondly, that it was through analysing inter-subjective interaction and engagement within this environment that norm diffusion could be understood (Katzenstein 1996a: 26). Attention was thereby drawn to the area of norm and identity construction as a way of explaining liberalizing shifts towards shared global norms that appeared not to fit traditional power- or interest-based understandings of government rationality or interests. The transitions of the Soviet bloc and the ending of apartheid in South Africa in the early 1990s seemed to offer strong evidence that subjective and ideational factors were much more important than material or structural understandings of fixed interests (see, for example, Harrison 2004; Thomas 2001; Black 1999). The importance given to the agential social construction of meanings, practices and identities in the international sphere reflected a fundamental shift in the study of international relations, which had previously understood the international sphere to be distinct from domestic society precisely because of a lack of shared meanings or interests (for an overview, see Bull 1977).

While 'first generation' agency-based theorists often stated that the fact that interests were socially constructed did not make them unimportant, the success of constructivism was based on the understanding that declarations of domestic, state or national 'interests' could no longer be taken as 'natural' or 'given'. If the structuring ideological 'interests' of Soviet states, in their opposition to liberal democracy, could seemingly collapse overnight, it was clear that no claim of legitimate 'interest' could withstand the sociological 'interpretivist' critique of rationalism (see, for example, Hollis and Smith 1990). In this framework, resistance to democratic or human rights norms on the basis of collectivist 'Asian values' was roundly dismissed as illegitimate (see, for example, Sen 1997; Parekh 2000; Donnelly 1998: 131–5). The prioritizing of international 'sociological' norms over discourses of exogenous state 'interests' was understood as a radical, critical stance towards the traditional framings of the state in international relations theorizing, and this assessment was questioned increasingly rarely as the sociological turn to theorizing agential choice became part of the policy and academic mainstream as the 1990s progressed.

Agency and communicative norms

The 'second wave' of agency-based thinking on liberal norms promotion, which developed in the mid- to late 1990s, raised the barrier of problematic agency. However, this was not yet the human-centred agency of the vulnerable and those who lacked adequate capacities to embrace external necessity. Here the barriers to change were understood to be the rational product of self-interest. Particular emphasis was placed upon the problematic agency of select non-Western state elites, while the understanding of positive or progressive agency shifted to focus upon (largely Western) non-state norm entrepreneurs. Martha Finnemore and Kathryn Sikkink developed a model of a 'norm life cycle', stressing the role of policy experts and networks of non-state actors in the emergence of liberal norms and in establishing their broad acceptance: in setting off 'norm cascades' (Finnemore and Sikkink 1998: 902–4). This framework relied on an alternative understanding of a non-atomistic, communicative rationality, heavily influenced by the work of Jürgen Habermas (see Brown 1994). This endogenous framing of an emerging and inclusive international society assumed that all state regimes or actors were equally capable of engaging in the communicative global realm and had the rational (and moral) capabilities to choose to follow these emerging liberal global norms.[6]

Finnemore and Sikkink referred to the development of 'world time', as increased global interdependence and the spread of communication and transportation links led to an increasing global interconnectedness. This increased connectedness, they suggested, had not just led to the 'homogenization of global norms' but also to the 'speed of normative change' and the success of 'norm entrepreneurs' in their rapid 'cascading' of global norms (Finnemore and Sikkink 1998: 909). It was the intensity of global communicative interaction which enabled liberal norms to spread through persuasion rather than coercion. Constructivist theorists stressed that:

> Networks of NGOs and intergovernmental organizations (IGOs) dealing with powerful states, however, are rarely able to 'coerce' agreement to a norm – they must persuade ... This process is not necessarily or entirely in the realm of reason, though facts and information may be marshalled to support claims. Affect, empathy, and principled moral beliefs may also be deeply involved, since the ultimate goal is not to challenge the 'truth' of something, but to challenge whether it is good, appropriate, and deserving of praise. (Ibid.: 900)

Under these assumptions, intersubjective engagement or communicative action enabled the spread of norms as local and parochial understandings of interests became transformed into universal, shared liberal understandings (Habermas 1997). It was upon this basis that globalization was seen to bring actors into dialogue in ways which enabled global liberal norms to diffuse as new global identities arose (see, for example, the World Bank publication, Martinsson 2011). The actions of any state elites, in blocking or opposing liberal reforms, were therefore held to be a product of their illegitimate, mistaken, criminal or short-sighted perceptions of their self-interests.[7] Despite the condemnation or criminalization of these actions, the agency of blocking state elites was seen as a product of bounded but rational self-interest rather than a vulnerability stemming from a lack of capacity.

Keck and Sikkink's influential book *Activists beyond Borders* argued that, to diffuse liberal norms of good governance and human rights, these illegitimate state-based or interest-based barriers to communicative interaction needed to be removed. These barriers were understood along similar lines to Habermas: the limit to the diffusion of norms was the unwillingness of actors to engage in communicative reason (see, for example, Habermas 1996). For many constructivist theorists, the focus was less on the US resistance to the spread of liberal democratic norms than the alleged reluctance of non-Western states, which were perceived as being most hostile because they had the most to lose from no longer being able to hide behind the 'impunity' that ruling elites claimed despite their unelected or non-democratic hold on power (see, for example, Robertson 1999).

The overcoming of barriers, seen to be at the level of state government resistance, was the work of the 'boomerang effect', which allowed the spread of liberal norms as international actors 'removed the blockage' of the narrow interest-based action of repressive regimes, 'prying open space' for domestic civil society actors which were bearers of these global liberal aspirations (Keck and Sikkink 1998: 12–13):

> Voices that are suppressed in their own countries may find that networks can project and amplify their concerns into an international arena, which in turn can echo back into their own countries … networks open channels for bringing alternative visions and information into international debate … At the core of network activity is the production, exchange and strategic use of information. (Ibid.: x)

In this discourse, all that was needed was the removal of narrow 'interest' blockages of entrenched power elites and the freeing of the agency of the rational subject. This framing was perhaps most exemplified by those advocating international intervention in the break-up of Yugoslavia, particularly in the Bosnia war of 1992–95, which was one of the key foreign policy focuses of the mid-1990s. It was held that international interveners were acting in support of local civil society actors in seeking to preserve multicultural Bosnia against the machinations of unrepresentative nationalist elites who were acting in their own narrow and criminal interests (see, for example, Burg 1997; Kaldor 1999; Fine 1996). Once international intervention had removed the nationalist leaders from power, through prosecutions for war crimes and the oversight of free and fair post-war democratic elections, it was assumed that the population of Bosnia would express their support for universal liberal norms in voting for non-nationalist political representatives.[8]

In the 1990s, the spread of liberal norms was understood on the basis that there were no insuperable barriers to an inclusive global community of communicative interaction and therefore the only limits to liberal norm diffusion were elite- or state-based barriers to communication. In this way, it was argued that the communicative interactions of transnational activist networks could 'bridge the increasingly artificial divide between international and national realms' (Keck and Sikkink 1998: 4). In many ways, this understanding of the role of Habermasian communicative interaction and the emergence of a global communicative space mirrored the understandings of critical global civil society theorists, such as Andrew Linklater, Mary Kaldor and John Keane (see, for example, Acharya 2000; Linklater 1998; Kaldor 2003; Keane 2003), who similarly juxtaposed the counterproductive or irrational understandings of elite self-interest to the progressive spread of an inclusive global communicative rationality.

Norms and behavioural modification

The 'second generation' of agency-based theorizing claimed to offer a set of explanations for the apparent triumph of liberal internationalist norms in the 1990s. However, it tended to be less able to explain the limits to the agentic dynamic of liberal norm diffusion, which became increasingly apparent in the late 1990s and into the 2000s. From the late 1990s onwards, this 'second generation' approach was criticized as positing an idealistic, normative, liberal teleology, where it was assumed that 'good' liberal ideas won out through intersubjective discourse (Hopgood 2000; Palan 2000; Chandler 2001, 2004). The concern with the limits of norm diffusion reflected an increased disillusionment with liberal internationalism – expressed in the setbacks and extensions to international protectorates in Bosnia (and later in Kosovo) and the disappointing outcomes of the wars fought under the rubric of the global war on terror in Afghanistan and Iraq (see, for example, Newman et al. 2009; Richmond and Franks 2009; Tadjbakhsh 2011; Campbell et al. 2011). In these states, it seemed that removing elites through war crimes prosecutions or regime change had not 'freed' society's civil or democratic forces, enabling populations to freely choose universal liberal norms. The focus inevitably shifted from the elite or state level to that of societal agency itself and the problem of individual and communal capacities.[9]

Current, societal, or 'third generation' norms research has tended to focus upon the differential agent-based understandings of the normative frameworks of domestic states and societies: the historical experiences and community and culture of the norm-blocking subject (see, for example, Acharya 2000). This discussion of the limits of liberal norm diffusion shifted the emphasis from the external diffusion of norms in the communicative space of global civil society to the internal reception of norms in the domestic institutional context, particularly that of the post-conflict, fragile or failing non-Western state. Thomas Risse, Stephen Ropp and Kathryn Sikkink's *The Power of Human Rights* was one of the first books to stake out this shift in sociological perspective (Risse et al. 1999). Rather than celebrating the power of global norms to have a transformative liberalizing impact, regardless of the 'geographic, cultural, and political diversity' of the countries studied, they choose instead to focus on the problematic limits to liberal norms in countries where it appeared that the democratic rights situation had worsened in the 1990s (Risse and Sikkink 1999: 3).

Making an important move, Risse, Ropp and Sikkink argued that the process of norm diffusion was more problematic than just facilitating free communicative links through removing irrational or illegitimate elite blockages.[10] Communicative engagement was not necessarily enough if the institutional frameworks shaping the understanding and behaviour of actors did not enable them to be open to communicative reason. It is from within this framing that the concepts of 'exclusion' and 'vulnerability' are derived: just as the excluded had to be included in order to take advantage of shared liberal values, so the vulnerable had to be empowered. In contexts of exclusion and vulnerability, blockages to 'freedom' were to be removed. Where this was the case, institutions held to be barriers to freedom, and the understandings and behaviours associated with them, first had to be changed. Risse, Ropp and Sikkink posed this process in terms of the 'spiral effect': the process through which modes of behaviour and understanding could be changed through external pressure, and the changing of institutional structures, eventually enabling global liberal norms to be accepted through free communicative interaction (Risse et al. 1999).

Rather than the power of liberal norms alone, Risse and Sikkink argued that 'domestic structural changes' were in some cases necessary to enable the spread of liberal norms (Risse and Sikkink 1999: 4). With the shift in emphasis to why liberal 'norms and principled ideas "do not float freely"' (an emphasis largely avoided in earlier discussions of 'global' norms), the focus shifted to the 'very different domestic structures' and 'rationalities' of states and societies having problems receiving or taking liberal norms (ibid.: 4). In discussing the limits to liberal norms, there was increasing sensitivity to blockages not at the level of the state but at the level of broader societal vulnerability or incapacity. Mere communicative interaction with international liberal norms was no longer adequate for norm diffusion if there was no shared communicative framework owing to the lack of adequate 'existing collective understandings' or adequate 'political cultures' (Risse and Ropp 1999: 271).

This framework of understanding internal cultural or ideational differences as preventing intersubjective dialogue from diffusing liberal norms should not be understood as a return to earlier understandings of rationalist or economistic perspectives with fixed interests and identities playing the determining role. In dealing with these 'blockages', Risse and Ropp, for example, argued that external pressure was necessary to get not just governments but societies to change their normative expectations of behaviour. Recalcitrant non-Western elites had to be coerced in order to take up liberal norms: 'Norm-violating governments tactically adjust to the new international discourse in order to stay in power, receive foreign aid, and the like' (ibid.: 273). However, the coercive understanding of the need for intervention to remove or transform the behaviour of domestic elites was not in itself the solution. The important point about the 'spiral approach' was that the focus shifted to the coercive or top-down transformation of social ideational frameworks.

Here, there was no assumption of 'freeing' the non-Western subject from elite- or state-based constraints: the emphasis was upon the transformation of the mind-sets of target societies or populations. The coercive intervention, to transform the actions or behaviour of elites, became important only insofar as it was a means to effect state policy changes that sought to change the behaviour and expectations of society itself. Societal ideational change became the goal rather than changing the self-understanding of state elites.[11] In terms of understanding the consequences of human-centred understandings of the self-production of society, it is important to highlight the assumption that societal ideational change will not be a matter of engagement in communicative reason – i.e. will not be merely a matter of freeing or liberalizing domestic economic and political frameworks – but rather a matter of enforcing behavioural change as the precondition for the later or subsequent 'free' acceptance of global liberal norms:

> we find that a different logic of interaction incrementally takes over and at least supplements strategic behaviour. This logic emphasizes communicative rationality, argumentation, and persuasion, on the one hand, and norm institutionalization and habitualization, on the other. We feel that social constructivism, which endogenizes identities and interests of actors, can accommodate this logic more easily, in conjunction with sociological institutionalism ... (Ibid.: 273)

This shift to the emphasis on 'norm institutionalization and habitualization' is of fundamental importance for understanding how social constructivist frameworks have facilitated and legitimized much more coercive and interventionist practices of international norms promotion. When endogenously generated norms (at the global level) were understood as progressive and transformative, actor agency was celebrated and seen as morally courageous. However, once endogenously generated norms were seen as barriers to progress (at the local level) agency then became problematized and actors were seen to be vulnerable in their lack of capacity for choice-making, resulting in the dangerous choosing and reproducing of 'immoral', 'reactionary' or 'non-liberal' norms.[12]

In these frameworks, the institutionalization of problematic norms necessitates external intervention to remove vulnerabilities and to engineer different ideational possibilities or subject capabilities. Institutional interventions to change 'everyday' practices and ideas are thus understood as a precondition for changes in agents' receptiveness to global liberal norms. It is only once institutional changes are made, and domestic actors transform their modes of understanding, that liberal norms become the subject of communicative rationality – or 'true dialogue' – and can become institutionalized as a new habitual practice (Risse and Sikkink 1999: 34). It is at this point that the liberal values, asserted to be essential to enabling peace and progress, can be understood as 'sustainable' and self-reproducing. It is important to emphasize this flip-side to the constructivist emphasis on the relationship of discursive equality – held to be in play to explain the transmission and spread of liberal norms. This is that the barriers to the spread of these norms are then understood to legitimize a shift from communicative reasoning to external intervention and behaviour modification. This external intervention is understood to be not oppressive but emancipatory: the basis upon which the post-conflict or post-colonial subject can be enlightened and placed in a position of self-liberation.[13]

One clearly formulated example of this approach, arguing for behavioural changing interventions in order to create the conditions for 'true dialogue' and thereby for the sustainability of liberal norm reproduction, is that of Roland Paris's conception of 'Institutionalization before Liberalization' (Paris 2004a). Paris maintains the constructivist understanding of the intersubjective construction of subject identity but argues that liberal internationalists have underestimated the societal blockages to rational choice-making and self-government. He argues that the introduction of liberal frameworks of governance and market social relations, rather than 'freeing' the non-Western subject, is highly problematic in societies with high levels of vulnerability and thereby lacking the right ideational and cultural preconditions. In effect, liberal freedoms are held to be problematic and counterproductive in societies understood to be unable to freely constitute themselves as liberal subjects. In these cases, the promotion of liberal norms involves the initial limiting of political and economic freedoms. External interventions have to act to regulate the political, social and economic spheres until behavioural and attitude changes allow the social acceptance of liberal norms. The dominant discourses of state-building and peace-building today operate on the basis of a critique of traditional liberal assumptions of the 'natural' or 'universal' subject. Human-centred discourses privilege difference above universality and understand the production of difference as the product of agential choice, whereby those who are vulnerable lack the capacities for adequate choice-making.

For the 'third generation' of agency-based understandings of norm diffusion, the subject has to be externally constituted before they can be 'free' to choose liberal values. For example, the lessons of the Balkans, the Middle East and of Africa are increasingly interpreted as the problem of 'too much' democracy rather than 'too little' (see, for example, Zaum 2007; Paris and Sisk 2009; Hawksley 2009). The title of Paul Collier's 2010 book, *Wars, Guns and Votes: Democracy in Dangerous Places*, sums up the increasing awareness that democracy promotion has to be done gradually and under the guidance of external interveners pursuing the new international state-building agendas of behavioural and ideational change, through extensive processes of societal intervention. Here, international relations theorists often pose the need to join with anthropologists to understand the societal reproduction of particular cultural vulnerabilities as institutional barriers to liberal norm diffusion (see, for example, Fukuyama 1995; Weldes et al. 1999).

The shrinking of the liberal world

As noted above, in the early 1990s sociological constructivists argued that they had made a fundamental break from rationalist or structuralist understandings of the limits of liberal norms, through positing the transformative nature of norm construction through agent-based communicative interaction.[14] Now it appeared that agency-based approaches could be just as useful in explaining the limits to change. However, introducing agential choice as a causal explanation for understanding the reproduction of ideational differences clearly lends itself to judgements made independently of the social, economic and political contexts in which norms are established. The concern with 'irrational' cultural or ideational mind-sets, as the explanation for differences in economic, social and political developments (see, for example, Hayek 1960; North 1990), had been a preoccupation of agent- and norms-based approaches outside the discipline of IR since, at least, the work of John R. Commons in the 1930s. For Commons, it was the system of shared understandings and behavioural expectations – agentically constructed norms – which explained the success of some countries and the lack of development of others (Commons 1936).[15]

Sociological approaches, bringing a variety of endogenously constructed frameworks of agentic explanation to bear on the reproduction of cultural and ideational barriers to the diffusion of liberal norms, have increasingly come to dominate the academic and policy agendas in the 2000s. This has particularly been the case in the fields of international peace-building and international state-building, where, as noted, the discourse has shifted from that of 'freeing' the subject from authoritarian regimes of regulation, to the prior overcoming of vulnerabilities through a broad range of societal interventions under the rubric of human-centred approaches to security and development (Chandler 2010b). These multi-level and multi-stakeholder initiatives are held to be necessary to enable the behavioural and ideational transformation of subjects through their participatory engagement in a wide range of policy activities (Belloni 2008; Chandler 1998; Paffenholz 2009). Other academic commentators have similarly focused on the 'hybrid' outcomes when there are attempts to impose global liberal norms on non- or aliberal societies, arguing, in effect, that the process of 'norm socialization' becomes blocked by countervailing practices and institutions (see, for example, Richmond 2011; Mac Ginty 2011; Roberts 2008; Barnett and Zürcher 2009).

Here, human-centred international relations theorizing, about liberal norms and the barriers to their promotion, lays stress on the cognitive and sociological institutional context in which shared meanings are produced and transmitted (see, for example, Acharya 2000; Tadjbakhsh 2011; Campbell et al. 2011). The call for more attention to the 'local' and even 'local-local' communicative transactions (see, for example, Richmond 2010), and to the specific cultural values and 'modes of life' of those in non-Western states and societies, may seem a radical or critical departure from traditional theorizing in international relations, but there are difficulties associated with the rejection of the universal rationalist assumptions of traditional liberal political science. Rationalist approaches tended to see ideas and choices as a product or reflection of rational interests, and therefore saw the structural or material socio-economic context as the key to addressing problems of difference and ideational contestation. Constructivist and other agency-based approaches, which eschew rationalist explanations, tend to explain differences in economic wealth or political institutions as the product of agentically constructed ideational structures and choices. In these approaches, the reproduction of difference is more likely to be understood as a product of vulnerable agential social or intersubjective construction than as shaped by material or structural social relations. As Douglass North, John Wallis and Barry Weingast put it:

The task of social science is to explain the performance characteristics of societies through time, including the radical gap in human well-being between rich countries and poor as well as the contrasting forms of political organization, beliefs, and social structure that produce these variations in performance. (North et al. 2009: 1)

For endogenous, human-centred approaches to social differentiation, the operation of market forces is no longer part of any causal explanation because material differences and social relations (though obviously important) are not, in themselves, adequate for explaining change but are often the product of pre-existing social institutional frameworks. Endogenous frameworks of thinking understand the world in terms of 'social orders', rather than economic orders, as they allege that social norms or social institutional frameworks are key to shaping individual behaviours which contribute to the perpetuation of differences and inequalities (see, for example, Thaler and Sunstein 2008). The key research questions then become the different patterns of social order, which enable theorists to explain the 'sociological' mystery of the political and economic limits of liberalism: why democratic norms are hard to promote, and 'why poor countries stay poor' (North et al. 2009: 3).

The agency-based approach to the problems of liberal limits was influentially articulated in development economics from the early 1970s (Davis and North 1971; North and Thomas 1973). One outstanding theorist in this area was Douglass C. North, the Nobel Prize-winning economist and leading World Bank policy adviser. Perhaps his best-known book, *Institutions, Institutional Change and Economic Performance* (1990), emphasized the importance not of formal government institutions (which were seen as relatively easy to change through external assistance) but informal institutions, particularly 'attitudes and ideologies'; concluding, in good sociological institutional fashion, that: 'Informal constraints matter. We need to know much more about culturally derived norms of behaviour and how they interact with formal rules to get better answers to such issues [of how social orders evolve]' (ibid.: 140).

In many ways, international relations was a disciplinary latecomer in rejecting rationalist framings, which is part of the reason why the transition away from realism (in many academic centres) occurred so rapidly and with relatively little disciplinary reflection (Peters 2005: 139). The shared theoretical frameworks with other agency-based, endogenous or institutionalist approaches in sociology, history and economics has meant that human-centred theorizing has been easily accommodated in mainstream institutional policy perspectives regarding the reconstruction of problems of conflict and poverty as subjectively constructed barriers to liberal norms. This can be usefully highlighted by surveying the dominance of endogenous perspectives concerning international problems and the ways in which these approaches operate to analyse the agentic social construction of limits to liberal norms.

At the *international level*, endogenous frameworks assert that state institutional arrangements construct vulnerabilities by cutting off their societies from access to the benefits of globalization (Ghani and Lockhart 2008). The need for international state-building as a framework of good governance is largely established on the basis that changes in state institutions can enable the mediation of the domestic and the international so that dysfunctional states can gain from global liberal norms and international institutional frameworks rather than being a threat to them. In fact, vulnerable, weak and failing states are often seen to constitute the major threat to the international order (see, for example, NSS 2002). Good governance promotion through state-building, as carried out by every major international institution from the EU to the UN and the World Bank, is seen to be capable of extending liberal norms through the human-centred focus on social empowerment with the use of external incentives and conditionalities: including the compacts proposed by a range of authors such as Ashraf Ghani, Clare Lockhart and Paul Collier (Ghani and Lockhart 2008; Collier 2010).

On the *state level*, endogenous approaches argue that culture and values – often agentically framed in the terminology of 'civil society' – are key to understanding the alleged barriers to the spread of liberal norms. Many of these arguments were cohered in the 1990s, in the discussion of the problem of 'transition' in the newly independent states in central and eastern Europe, where it was alleged that external assistance for institution-building was necessary to allow democracy and the market to work without conflict and disruption (see, for example, Fukuyama 1995; Schmitter and Karl 1991; O'Donnell 1996; Gunther et al. 1996). The problems of facilitating change or 'transition' are central to endogenous approaches to international development, where institutional path dependencies are held to constitute vulnerabilities preventing easy transitioning to liberal 'open-access' social orders (see, for example, North et al. 2009). In this framework, it is the ideas, values and social institutional culture of a society which appear to constitute subjects as vulnerable rather than the inequalities of economic wealth or hierarchical socio-economic relations (Collier 2010; Snyder 2000; Zakharia 2003).

On the *individual level*, endogenous approaches argue that individuals are inherently vulnerable in that we are all poorly equipped to deal with change and therefore tend to act on the basis of existing sociological institutional understandings and practices and individually shaped past experience. Douglass North, for example, draws heavily on the work of leading neoliberal theorist Friedrich Hayek (particularly Hayek 1952), to argue that evolutionary psychology provides the best framework for understanding the differential social construction of meaning and therefore the inequality of market economic outcomes:

> Culture not only determines societal performance at a moment in time but, through the way in which its scaffolding constrains the players, contributes to the process of change through time. The focus of our attention, therefore, must be on human learning – on what is learned and how it is shared among the members of society and on the incremental process by which the beliefs and preferences change, and on the way in which they shape the performance of economies through time. (North 2005: viii)

It therefore may seem that a note of caution is called for when transferring calls for greater attention to the agentic construction of culture, identity and values from the international level, where there had traditionally been little attention to these aspects of agency, to the level of the non-Western state. The idea that the barriers to liberal norms are endogenous, subjective, cultural or ideational products has a long tradition of being used to argue that differences cannot be easily overcome. Either this framing can easily result in an apologia for gross inequalities of outcomes or, just as problematically, for gross inequalities of treatment, justifying coercive interventions with the goal of social or ideational engineering. Social constructivism, along with other 'new institutionalist' approaches, has sought to eschew the racialized and culturalized framings of traditional 'institutionalist' sociological and historical approaches of the colonial era, which focused on the endogenous reproduction of societal difference (see Peters 2005: 1–24). I wish to suggest that a complete break with former colonializing approaches, which essentialized difference, is not possible within the framework of human-centred theorizing: that, in fact, the problems with this approach cannot be overcome by substituting the discourse of 'agentic norms' for that of race and culture. This is because the problematic of endogenous approaches necessarily involves certain shared methodological assumptions, which are drawn out in the section below.

The self-production of the vulnerable subject

The foregoing work has sought to highlight problems that are integral to endogenous frameworks of understanding as they seek to explain the limits to liberal norm promotion. It has highlighted these problems by specifically focusing on the most widely accepted framework for interrogating the spread of liberal norms: social constructivism. Endogenous approaches share two core problematic attributes, which have enabled social constructivism to act as a methodological framework through which policy and academic understandings of norm promotion have been able to shift from agential understandings of the international sphere (seen to be radical and progressive) to the potentially less radical and progressive problematization of non-Western societies as vulnerable and as producing or choosing to constitute barriers to the universalization of liberal norms. These attributes are, first, epistemological and, secondly, ontological.

The epistemological attribute which norm-based sociological understandings share with other new institutionalist or agent-based approaches, which also lack the foundational grounds of universalist rationalist and materialist approaches, is that they can only work backwards to explain the present. Agency-based understandings can easily account both for continuity and for change (Kowert and Legro 1996: 483). This all-purpose explanatory framework may not have seemed so problematic when liberal transformations, perceived as progressive, were being analysed with the fall of the Soviet Union and the 'domino effect' of democratic change in central and eastern Europe (Macdonald 1995; Jervis and Snyder 1991). However, it is certainly much more problematic when we are dealing with post hoc cultural, value- and identity-based understandings of the agentic reproduction of different ideas and policy preferences.[16] Part of this problem is that efforts to identify agency suffer from a bias towards 'the norm that worked' (Kowert and Legro 1996: 485). In the agency-based framings of constructivism, 'the norm that worked' is another way of saying 'the agency that worked'; for this reason agency was ascribed to non-state actors and norm entrepreneurs, well beyond their representative political influence or socio-economic power. Once the focus shifts to understanding the perpetuation of barriers to liberal norms, 'the norm that worked' gives agential power to those choosing, holding and reproducing non-liberal norms – often those with the least social, economic and political weight in non-Western states. In this case, it is not surprising that societies, understood as vulnerable, are seen to be complicit in the reproduction of their own frameworks of subjection and subordination.

The ontological attribute shared by both mainstream constructivist agency-based approaches and other new institutionalist approaches is that they can explain change (and the limits to change) only as internally generated (Kratochwil 2000: 97). In early constructivist approaches, this process inevitably marginalized or excluded the 'exogenous' processes taking place outside the global sphere of intersubjective communicative exchange between global actors. The boundaries between the domestic and the international were held to be increasingly blurring and this facilitated an understanding of a shared closed system, which more and more approximated to a dematerialized and discursive global level. From the globalizing of the international into a closed system capable of extending and reproducing liberal norms and values, the problematizing of liberal norm promotion has led to the construction of a conflicting and differentiated understanding dividing the international into liberal or resilient and non-liberal or vulnerable worlds. One world is held to choose the safe reproduction of liberal norms and ideas and the other world is held to choose the problematic reproduction of non-liberal norms and ideas. It is here that the focus on agency, rather than structure, forces constructivist understandings to see non-liberal values as a 'choice' made by vulnerable subjects.

This subjectivization of the limits of liberalism then leads theorists to see these vulnerable choices as either morally problematic, and thereby an indication of a subjective threat to be dealt with through policies of intervention, or alternatively as a subjective political act of resistance to be offered solidarity and understanding, on the basis that we all share in these vulnerablities. In either perspective the endogenous framework of agency-based understanding fits unerringly into the human-centred understanding that political, social and economic inequalities are a product of free choice-making, that, to paraphrase Wendt (1992): 'capitalism is what states make of it' or 'social welfare is what states make of it' or 'democracy is what states make of it'. Once the limits to liberal norm promotion become understood as subjective products of vulnerable or non-liberal subject choices – as we have seen – there is no longer any rationale for the promotion of liberal norms. Either these norms have to be imposed through interventions aimed at behaviour modification and social and ideational engineering, which necessitate the limiting of democratic and liberal freedoms of choice, or we have to express solidarity with, accept and learn from the non-liberal other and apparently appreciate that it chooses not to have, is not ready for or is too 'other' for liberal democratic freedoms.

Conclusion

Human-centred discourses, by maintaining that we create and institutionalize differences through our own agentic choices, constitute a world which can never be collectively engaged with. Rather than starting from a universalist position that human subjects are rational, even though the contexts and the structures in which we make choices and decisions are very different across time and space, the human-centred gaze sees only the individual (or community) constructing their own world through agential choice. The more the explanation for problems and for changes in the world is reduced to the decision-making choices of individuals, the less rational or understandable, and the more alien and exotic, the world becomes. We can never understand or be at home in this world, and in excluding ourselves from the world make ourselves poorer as a result.

As Ralph Waldo Emerson put it, we would be merely living a 'shallow village tale' (1993: 17) if we were not able to appropriate, to find ourselves in, the events of our world, both across time and space. We would lack any sense of our common humanity, our understanding of our past or our present, if we could not examine the history of the world and find not exoticism but the opposite, that: 'There is no age or state of society or mode of action in history, to which there is not somewhat corresponding in [one's] life' (ibid.: 3). This shared world of meaning and understanding is destroyed by agent-centred understandings. Emerson's universalist approach to the reading of history allows us to: 'assume that we under like influence should be like affected and should achieve the like; and we [could] aim to master intellectually the steps, and reach the same height or the same degradation, that our fellow, our proxy, has done' (ibid.: 4). Under the human-centred gaze, the problems of the world, from conflict to economic inequality and environmental degradation, become alien to us because we construct them as products of problematic, exotic and vulnerable agents whose thought processes we cannot understand, imagine or relate to.

In giving human agency centre place and in abolishing structures, agent-based understandings of new institutionalism and social constructivism remove the universalist liberal assumptions of rationalist approaches. For the advocates of this shift, the subject is liberated from the constrictions of structural frameworks. In this reading, change becomes possible once it is understood that the subject or agent can shape the processes of interaction in which they are embedded. If, as Wendt argued, 'the world is what agents make of it', the apparent disastrousness of the world appears to indicate that the human subject is not capable of very much and there is very little that we as human subjects can do about it apart from rejecting the liberal hubris of rationalism and making do with the world as it is. Once human-centred framings of the world place the human at the centre of the problematic, even radical agent-centred attempts to improve the world end up reinforcing the current internalized understanding of change, dictated by external necessity. Once we start from the problematic of the human – in terms of empowering or capacity-building the vulnerable – we inevitably ignore the external world, reducing the world to the human and the human to the cognitive processes of the human head and the environmental milieu of social institutions, norms and values which are held to influence and shape it. In the following chapter, the discourse of securing the human through societal interventions is drawn out further, particularly emphasizing how this framework transforms traditional understandings of autonomy and freedom in international relations.

6 | EMPOWERMENT AND HUMAN SECURITY

Introduction

In liberal discourses of international relations, international intervention was understood as undermining sovereign rights. In a world constructed in the legal and political framework of rights subjects, intervention and sovereignty were conceptual opposites: intervention denoted the denial of freedom and autonomy. This chapter is concerned with the shifting understanding of intervention under regimes of human-centred or post-liberal governance. In this framing, the world is no longer constructed on the liberal basis of rights subjects but sociologically around subjects understood to lack capabilities and therefore in need of empowerment. Discourses of intervention as empowerment operate on a different register (or grid of intelligibility) to liberal discourses, and are seen to operate at the societal level rather than the international political or legal level. In the chapter which follows, discourses of human security will be analysed to highlight that it is in this area that the shift to the societal level has enabled discussions of international intervention to go beyond the disputed conceptions of humanitarian intervention and the 'responsibility to protect' in liberal constructions of the 1990s.

The key point which will be made here is that the shift towards human-centred approaches to security and development can usefully be understood as in part to have evolved in response to the 1990s – a decade shaped by liberal internationalist discourses of humanitarian intervention and the restrictions of the rights of sovereignty. This shift away from 1990s conceptions of intervention is drawn out through a close examination of the discursive framing of human security. The chapter will suggest that it is within this framework of security that human- and agent-centred approaches became fully articulated. While the 'human' was invoked in the 1990s discussions of human rights and of the rights of humanitarian intervention, agency was ascribed to the international actors and institutions understood to be acting to secure these rights and to be protecting others. It is only with human security approaches that we see international policy interventions operate in a different register – the one concerned with in this book – which places the agency of the 'other' at the centre of policy debates and of proposed policy interventions.

Human security

In the 1990s and 2000s, debates over human security focused largely upon whether human security discourses were a challenge to the hierarchies of power – focusing on the holistic concerns of economic, social and political security, particularly the needs of the most marginal – or were instead liable to become co-opted into Western security agendas legitimizing external military intervention and undermining state sovereignty. An alternative reading is sketched out here, which suggests that debates over 'narrow' or 'broad' human security frameworks have under-theorized the discursive paradigm at the heart of human security. This reading draws out the juxtaposition of preventive security practices of resilience, working upon the vulnerable, and interventionist security practices of protection, working upon victims. It is suggested that human security can be conceptually analysed in terms of post-intervention, as a shift away from Western claims of securing agency and towards a concern with the securing agency of those held to be the most vulnerable. In this manner, human security discourses evade liberal rights-based, legal and political understandings of intervention, reinterpreting the practices of intervention in terms of empowerment and capacity- and capability-building rather than as acts of sovereign power and the limiting of autonomy.

International intervention into (post-)conflict zones has been radically transformed since the high-profile debates and discussions of humanitarian intervention and human rights in the 1990s. In that decade, the dominant discursive framings were those of abusers and victims – and the insertion of international interveners in the role of external saviours and external judges, with the moral duty of bringing security and the sovereign rule of law to the benighted borderlands. In this framework, non-Western victims were to be protected or saved by humanitarian interveners who assumed the role of sovereign protection once the post-colonial or post-conflict state was judged to lack the capacities or the will to fulfil its sovereign duties of protecting the human rights and security of its citizens. Security was to be constructed in the universal human-rights-centred language of cosmopolitan law, rather than in the state-based, territorialized language of international relations, where it was held that governing elites could hide behind claims to sovereign impunity. Sovereignty had to give way to intervention in order for a new world of global rights and global security to be enforced (see, for example, Archibugi 2000; Booth 1991; Linklater 1998).

Allied to the discussions of humanitarian intervention and the protection of human rights, a third 'human-centred' framework entered international policy discourse in the mid-1990s: that of human security. Human security frameworks were posed in less clear terms – with an emphasis on prevention and international development, under the rubric of 'freedom from want', providing a much broader and more encompassing framework of securing the human (Watson 2011). From this vantage point, the narrower, more reactive and more coercive frameworks of humanitarian intervention, under the rubric of 'freedom from fear', could be softened through stressing the less militarized aspects of international engagement. In this way, human security appeared to try to saddle two horses at once, creating confusion or ambiguity as to whether the concept should be broadly or narrowly construed (Martin and Owen 2010: 213–14). Nevertheless, both 'narrow' (more conservative) and 'broad' (more radical) approaches were understood as presaging a transformation in international security approaches, challenging the traditional agendas of power and placing the needs of the individual at the centre of security discourses (Kaldor 2007; Tadjbakhsh and Chenoy 2007).

Human security was often seen as the least conceptually interesting of the three 'human-centred' framings, lacking the overt political and legal content of the discussion of the rights of humanitarian intervention against the sovereign rights of statehood. In fact, it was held that the ambiguity of the concept meant that, unlike the rights discourses, with their contested and potentially clarifying nature, human security could mean 'all things to all men' (see Paris 2004a; Buzan 2004; Mack 2004). This chapter argues that the conceptual power of human security discourses and their capacity to reshape policy frameworks has often been underestimated (Chandler 2008). One reason for this is the fact that academic and policy discourses of human security have tended to be highly reductionist. Often debate and discussion have focused upon whether there is a synergy or a policy conflict between the 'softer' (or 'broader') security concerns of economic and social well-being – 'the freedom from want' – and the 'harder' (or 'narrower') security concerns of military intervention to protect populations from human rights abuses – 'the freedom from fear'. This reductionist view has been encouraged by the concept's advocates, who have argued that there is indeed such a synergy between 'broad' and 'narrow' conceptions as part of a holistic approach to human security (Ogata n.d.; Alkire 2004; Thomas 2004). This framing has been reinforced by the concept's critics, who have articulated a crude binary division between a military/security focus held to reinforce dominant power relations and a development/basic needs focus held to be a radical challenge to dominant power relations (Roberts 2009; see also Chandler and Hynek 2011).

A variant of this view of the binary between the coercive 'narrow' view of human security and the progressive 'broader' perspective is the argument that human security itself is becoming marginalized with the growing dominance of security concerns under the rubric of the Responsibility to Protect (R2P), with its emphasis on the military and coercive powers of Western states rather than upon the economic and social needs of populations (see, for example, Orford 2011). This perspective is clearly articulated in an article in *International Affairs*, by Mary Martin and Taylor Owen, who argue that the term human security 'has all but vanished' from high-level UN reports (2010: 211) and that security discourses are now dominated by the R2P, with its emphasis on military intervention and the conditional nature of sovereignty. They argue that this shift has denuded the radical content of human security approaches to the point where it is no longer clear whether international interventions are serving the broader economic, social and political security needs of others or promoting Western security interests through projecting power abroad to ensure stability (ibid.: 222).

This binary division is emphasized in the 2010 UN secretary-general's *Human Security* report to the General Assembly, which clearly distances human security from the concerns of the use of force, now seen to be firmly the prerogative of the R2P:

> The use of force is not envisaged in the application of the human security concept. The focus of human security is on fostering Government and local capacities and strengthening the *resilience* of both to emerging challenges in ways that are mutually reinforcing, *preventive* and comprehensive.

Meanwhile the responsibility to *protect*, as agreed upon by Member States in paragraphs 138 to 140 of the World Summit Outcome, focuses on *protecting* populations from specific cases of genocide, war crimes, ethnic cleansing and crimes against humanity. (UNSG 2010: §23–4, emphases added)

In this framing, human security is demarcated from the use of force (see also Kaldor 2011) as a separate set of broader non-coercive practices defined in terms of a preventive framework of strengthening resilience at the level of both the post-conflict state and society. I have added emphases to the above quote, in order to flag up the preventive discourse of resilience as key to human security vis-à-vis post hoc intervention to protect victims of human rights abuses. This chapter will focus on these aspects of intervention rather than on the demarcation of the potential use of force referred to in the passage.

Several claims will be staked out in this chapter, relating to the underlying conceptual framing of the divisions established between 'freedom from want' and 'freedom from fear', also articulated in terms of the divide between human security approaches and the R2P:

- The first claim is that the reductionist division between these approaches has focused on the distinction between social and economic concerns and military concerns at the expense of a conceptual understanding of the nature and meaning of intervention itself. It will be suggested that a more useful distinction would be between the paradigms of resilience and protection. The resilience paradigm clearly puts the agency of those most in need of assistance at the centre, stressing a programme of empowerment and capacity-building, whereas the protection paradigm puts the emphasis upon the agency of external interveners, acting to protect or to secure the victims of state-led or state-condoned abuses. The discursive power of human security stems from its articulation of the resilience paradigm vis-à-vis the protection paradigm and has facilitated the shift in dominant discourses from the emphasis on protection in the 1990s to a growing emphasis on resilience in the 2000s.
- Secondly, it will be suggested that, once the reductionist binaries are put aside, the distinction between social-economic and military engagements becomes less important, while the more important questions concern how these international practices operate.

Military intervention can be discursively framed as empowering and capacity-building just as economic and social provision can be framed in terms of protection. These points will be drawn out later in the chapter with regard to the R2P and the bombing of Libya and overthrow of President Muammar Gaddafi in 2011.

- Third, this chapter claims that once the conceptual distinctions at the heart of human security discourses are drawn out, it seems clear that rather than being undermined by concerns with the R2P, human security framings are predominant in academic and policy security discourses.

This chapter conceptualizes human security in terms of the resilience paradigm of post-intervention (see, further, Chandler 2010a; Foucault 2008; Joerges 2010; Walker and Cooper 2011). The conceptual framing of post-interventionism seeks to demarcate human security frameworks from those of humanitarian intervention based on the reaction to abuses and the protection of victims; in a post-interventionist/resilience paradigm, the emphasis is on prevention rather than intervention, empowerment rather than protection, and work upon the vulnerable rather than upon victims. Seeing human security as a discourse of post-intervention concerned with the inculcation of resilience heuristically enables an analysis of human security which does not rely on the 'word-search' approach favoured by authors who point to the rise or the decline of human security merely upon the basis of the frequency of the term in official documents and reports. Focusing upon the emergence of post-interventionist framings of security, it will be suggested that the decline of human security as a policy paradigm has been much exaggerated.

Shifting paradigms of security

This section focuses on the R2P and, in the heuristic terms of paradigm shifts, draws out two stages: first, the shift towards a global discursive framework of intervention posed in terms of the weighing of competing concerns of human rights and sovereignty – reflected in debates on the 'right of intervention' and the alleged emergence of a 'global community' capable of authorizing such intervention – which was dominant in the 1990s; followed by a retreat from the consequences of this liberal internationalist imaginary, to what is described here as the post-interventionist paradigm, cohered in the

2000s, which moved beyond the liberal problematic, reformulating the political subject in relation to security in terms of resilience (the need to intervene to construct securing capacity) rather than autonomy (the capacity to secure oneself). In this framework, the inculcation of resilience is the work of external engagement conceived in post-interventionist terms, as prevention rather than as post hoc intervention. In this way, intervention and sovereignty are no longer binary opposites; there is no longer an inside and an outside or a clash of rights. Human security approaches reflect a shift in international policy away from an interventionist approach held to challenge states and to undermine sovereignty. In this framework, intervention is reconceived as essential to the construction of securing agency or securing subjects: as an act of empowerment rather than an act of external power.

Interventionism of the 1990s In the 1990s, with the collapse of the Cold War divide, many theorists and political leaders suggested that the end of the problematic of IR had been reached with the domestication of the global. States began to articulate 'ethical' foreign policies, eschewing the idea of national interests and articulating the values of 'global citizenship'. In this 'new international order', leading Western states suggested that, in the absence of a formally constituted global sovereign, they could act as putative sovereigns of the international sphere. Through discussions of human rights protection and humanitarian intervention, leading policy discourses of the international framed the world in liberal terms, whereby Western states and international institutions, such as the United Nations, NATO, the OSCE and the European Union, increasingly came to envisage international policy-making as if they were acting not merely as representatives of their own interests but as imagined global authorities, capable of securing and protecting the lives and interests of others.

In this context, the boundaries of sovereignty appeared not to matter, and Western governments began to conceive of domestic and foreign policies in similar terms, regardless of representation or accountability (see, for example, Cooper 2003). In the terminology of Michel Foucault, the international sphere was imagined as a 'liberal economy of power' in which freedom and security could be framed similarly in both the domestic and international arenas. The question of 'intervention' was calculated on the basis of this balance:

The principle of calculation is what is called security. That is to say, liberalism, the liberal art of government, is forced to determine the precise extent to which and up to what point individual interest, that is to say individual interests insofar as they are different and possibly opposed to each other, constitute a danger for the interest of all. (Foucault 2008: 65)

The particular freedoms of state sovereignty were weighed against the collective security of 'international society', held to be manifest in the duty of protecting the rights and security of all. Security discursively shifted from a concern of states, with the protection and promotion of their national interests, to the interventionist discourse of human rights protection, construed as a reflection of the immanent or emerging 'global community'.

The liberal framing of the international sphere imagined the domestication of conflict under the regulatory gaze of the putative global sovereigns, acting with or without the consent of the UN Security Council, as representatives of an immanent, global legal framework (see, for example, Held 1995; Archibugi 2003; Kaldor 2003; Habermas 1999). The ability of major Western powers to intervene began to be equated with a moral legitimacy to act in accordance with higher laws, articulated over the NATO war over Kosovo, in terms of 'natural law', 'cosmopolitan law' or 'global ethics' (see AJIL 1999; Krish 2002).

However, the assertive and optimistic mood of the 1990s began to dissipate as the putative claims to global sovereignty resulted in a counter-discourse of Western responsibility. If the West was now responsible, why was it that troops were not dispatched to prevent genocide in Rwanda? Why did Western states prevaricate and delay when intervention was needed to prevent genocide in Bosnia? Why was it that the war over Kosovo, the asserted high-water mark of global liberal interventionism, was fought from 15,000 feet, preventing the loss of a single NATO life but at the cost of the 'collateral' damage of the deaths of many of those whom NATO was sent to save? Why was it that global responsibility seemed to stop when it came to addressing the structural inequalities of poverty and insecurity that blighted whole swathes of the post-colonial world, especially sub-Saharan Africa? The political leaders of Western states and international institutions realized that the discourse of global ethics and Western responsibility had its limits: that the consequences of dismissing the importance of international law and sovereign statehood undermined, rather than enforced, their moral claims to global leadership. It was in the context of the rolling back of liberal interventionist claims of Western responsibility, and of the overt claims of Western powers to the mantle of global sovereignty, that the R2P concept emerged. Perhaps counterintuitively, the R2P was taken up as a response designed to limit claims upon the West: as a retreat from Western responsibility. With the R2P, the focus of agency began to shift away from the responsibility of 'great power' to secure others to the agency or 'resilience' of those lacking the power to secure themselves.

The retreat from intervention The conceptual roots of the R2P lie in Francis Deng's assertion of 'Sovereignty as Responsibility' in response to superpower post-Cold War withdrawal from Africa and the need to constitute local and regional forms of conflict management as a substitute for the USA taking responsibility (see Deng et al. 1996). This conceptual framing was drawn upon when the R2P was formally conceived in 2000, in the wake of the Kosovo campaign; when Western states, under the banner of the NATO alliance, launched a humanitarian intervention without the consent of the UN Security Council. The International Commission on Intervention and State Sovereignty (ICISS), which produced the *Responsibility to Protect* report in 2001, sought to deflect attention from Western responsibility and Western rights of intervention, arguing that responsibility for the protection of basic rights and security was shared but was primarily the responsibility of the domestic state concerned (ICISS 2001a). Starting from the functional responsibility to protect the individual, the report steered away from the liberal discourse of intervention and protection, which pitted the universal 'human' rights of individuals against the particularist, conditional, sovereign rights of states.

Defining the protection of rights as the responsibility of sovereignty, the report argued that there was no clash of rights and that Western states had responsibilities to facilitate the sovereign capacities of non-Western states, and only if this failed would coercive intervention be necessary. The Commission's report can be usefully understood as a conscious attempt to mediate the relationship between Western responsibility and the problems of conflict in the non-Western world while reassuring the advocates of Western intervention that 'bringing the non-Western state back in' was not a retreat from 1990s aspirations for peace and order. The Commission sought to distance itself from the liberal interventionist arguments of those who claimed that the Western intervention was essentially without sovereign limits, and amounted to no more than 'cosmopolitan law enforcement', more akin to domestic policing than international realpolitik (see Kaldor 2003).

The R2P reflected a world where the liberal discourse of the globalizing or domestication of the international sphere shifted on to the defensive and clearly articulated the signs of retreat from the triumphal claims of the early and mid-1990s (see Chandler 2006). However, for the advocates of the R2P, it was understood, at the time, as representing and institutionalizing the gains of that era. It was seen to be a symbol of the global cosmopolitan order of liberal rights and justice, which the 1990s appeared to promise. For these advocates, the evolution of the R2P has been a disappointment and hard to explain (see, for example, Evans 2008; Bellamy 2009). Why has the interventionist promise of the R2P been muted? Why did the UN World Summit agreement of 2005 entirely separate R2P from the need to reform the decision-making process of intervention in the UN Security Council?

The rise of a post-interventionist order The inner logic of the R2P, as a reflection of the shift from the paradigm of intervention, was explicitly drawn out when the concept was revived by Kofi Annan in 2003, in preparation for the World Summit (Evans 2008; Bellamy 2009; Chandler 2009b). Prevention, rather than being a secondary concern, became the primary focus as the locus of securing agency shifted from Western actors to the fragile or failing states in need of capacity-building. This reformulation as a bottom-up, more 'empowering' approach to human security was constructed on the basis of an agent-centred understanding of conflict and underdevelopment in the non-Western world (see, for example, North 1990; World Bank 1997, 2000; Ghani and Lockhart 2008). The UN secretary-general's follow-up report to the World Summit illustrated this approach well in asking the question 'why one society plunges into mass violence while its neighbours remain relatively stable' (UNSG 2009: para. 15). The answer it provided was the agent-centred one, focusing on individuals as decision-makers and upon their immediate choice-making influences rather than upon economic and social relations. From this starting position, the problematic becomes one of how to empower or capacity-build agents (on an individual and societal basis) to enable them to overcome their vulnerabilities and therefore become more resilient:

> Genocide and other crimes relating to the responsibility to protect do not just happen. They are, more often than not, the result of a deliberate and calculated political choice, and of the decisions and actions of political leaders who are all too ready to take advantage of existing social divisions and institutional failures. (Ibid.: para. 21)

The understanding of mass atrocities as a product of individual choices and immediate institutional shortcomings then sets up the agenda for international preventive engagement to assist in institutional capacity-building that would inculcate resilience and make states 'less likely to travel the path to crimes relating to the responsibility to protect':

> Experience and common sense suggest that many of the elements of what is commonly accepted as good governance – the rule of law, a competent and independent judiciary, human rights, security sector reform, a robust civil society, an independent press and a political culture that favours tolerance, dialogue and mobility over the rigidities of identity politics – tend to serve objectives relating to the responsibility to protect as well. (Ibid.: para. 44)

Here, there was no liberal internationalist discourse of protecting the victims. There was no 'quick fix' of intervention and exit strategies, but a much more long-term programme of prevention. This 'broader' and more empowering focus on prevention reflected disillusionment with the 1990s promise of Western solutions and reflected a set of much lower expectations. These lower expectations were expressed through the stress upon differences between institutions and cultures, which constituted a barrier to any Western capacity to protect or to assume securing responsibilities (see, further, Chandler 2012). The best that the international community could do was merely to indirectly work to facilitate good governance mechanisms and capacity-build societal institutions, which were seen as the ultimate solution. This framing, focusing on agential causes rather than the humanitarian consequences, reflected a broader shift in the understanding of the World Bank and other international development agencies that economic and social problems in post-conflict and post-colonial states could not be addressed merely by the provision of Western aid and resources (World Bank 1997, 2000). The causes of insecurity were not seen to be poverty per se but rather the institutional frameworks through which broader security concerns were managed (see Sen 1999; Commission for Africa 2005). Agent-centred approaches have been central to the development of human security, based on the rejection of direct attempts to address problems through the provision of external social, economic and military resources, of the sort associated with post hoc or responsive protection. It was held that the provision of resources would be inadequate as a response and could make problems worse if the underlying causes of conflict or insecurity, held to lie in the social institutional frameworks of agential choice, were not addressed.

Dealing with the problem of weak or failing states in the post-interventionist paradigm of human security does not rely on a liberal discourse of intervention – of the post hoc Western provision of solutions – whether in terms of eco-social provision or of military force. There is a paradigmatic difference between intervention posed in terms of post hoc protection with the assumption of sovereign power and the human security provision of preventive deployments of force, which lack the assumptions of undermining sovereignty and assuming responsibility. This shift was aptly demonstrated by the bombing of Libya in 2011, heralded by many international relations commentators as marking a return to the 1990s era of humanitarian intervention (Sewer 2011; Robertson 2011; Evans 2011). However, the dropping of bombs over Libya clearly lacked the ethical, political and legal framework of discussion of the 1990s. The Libya campaign did not present the 'humanitarian' bombing as an undermining of state sovereignty. There was no claim of external sovereign rights or that the international interveners assumed sovereign responsibility to protect the Libyan people. The no-fly zone and its extended enforcement were posed as facilitating the agency of the Libyan people, enabling then to begin the process of securing themselves. The campaign lasted substantially longer than the NATO war over Kosovo but lacked any of the meaning or clarity of objectives, which would have been necessary if any direct assumption of responsibility had been claimed. This ambiguity reflects the different paradigm of understanding at play in a 'war' fought without the claims of securing agency and sovereign responsibility. Libya illustrates how the human-centred discourse operates in a different register, dissolving the clarity of liberal security frameworks in the language of capacity-building and good governance. Human-centred interventions cannot be grasped in the legal and political terms of the 1990s, whereby intervention was conceived of in terms of a clash of legal and political rights and sovereign claims of securing agency.

Resilience: the agent-centred paradigm

The human-centred security order is conceptually analysed in very different terms from those of the 1990s debates, which pitched individual-centred against state-centred approaches. The agent-centred understanding no longer opposes external intervention to sovereignty as if this was a zero-sum game, or articulates intervention in the language of a clash of rights or as a problem which needs a legal solution. The human security practices operating under the paradigm of resilience cannot be grasped in terms of the clash of liberal rights, in the formal spheres of law or politics. Using an entirely different register, resilience operates conceptually by reinterpreting external intervention as productive of securing subjects. Inverting liberal assumptions of the foundational subject, human security does away with the liberal binary of intervention/non-intervention.

In this paradigm, the external management of, or intervention in, post-conflict or post-colonial state policy-making is understood as a process of empowerment, of capacity- and capability-building. This shift is reflected well in discussions of intervention as bridging the 'sovereignty gap' (Ghani et al. 2005) and in Stephen Krasner's view of 'domestic sovereignty' being built up (or co-produced) by external actors on the basis of giving up 'Westphalian/Vattelian sovereignty' (Krasner 2004: 87–8; see, further, Chandler 2010a). Despite the increased regulatory engagement, the discourse is one of prevention and the building of sovereignty, not of intervention and the denial of sovereignty. As demonstrated above, through reflection upon the R2P, our understanding of the international sphere has shifted from the 1990s, bringing discourses of 'freedom from fear' very much into line with the discourses of 'freedom from want' as articulated in the more 'radical' or empowering discourses of human security.

What this illustrates is that the framing of the 'broader' human security discourse is exactly that which facilitates dominant discourses of international regulation and intervention today, as opposed to the struggle to displace 'state-based' approaches to security with 'individual-centred' ones. Human security's articulation as a more progressive framework of security depends for its radical status upon the critique of liberal discourses of intervention posed in terms of sovereignty and rights. With the shift away from the liberal discourse of intervention, privileged in the 1990s, human security's claims to offer an alternative to mainstream approaches – through emphasizing the prevention, empowerment and the agency of the post-conflict and post-colonial subject – lose their basis. In fact, one reason why the words 'human security' may have dropped from mainstream discourse is that this conceptual framing of the questions and issues at stake has already been accepted.

From its inception, in the 1994 UNDP *Human Development* report, *New Dimensions of Human Security*, the conceptual framework of human security has always sat uneasily with the focus on sovereignty and intervention at the centre of discussions of the legal and political standing of humanitarian reasons for intervention. This can be seen quite clearly by consideration of the four 'essential characteristics' of human security flagged up as part of the radical rethinking of traditional state-based security frameworks: the first two are the fact that human security approaches are conceived as 'universal' and 'interdependent', the second two are that human security approaches focus on 'prevention' rather than intervention and that they are 'people-centred' (UNDP 1994: 22–33). There is no discussion about the problematic of sovereignty; in fact, from its inception human security discourses focused on people as agents, rather than as victims in need of protection, and upon intervention as a way of giving people more control over their own lives and of enhancing their autonomy:

> Ensuring human security does not mean taking away from people
> the responsibility and opportunity for mastering their lives. To
> the contrary, when people are insecure, they become a burden on
> society.
>
> The concept of human security stresses that people should be
> able to take care of themselves: all people should have the opportu-
> nity to meet their most essential needs and to earn their own living.
> This will set them free and help ensure that they can make a full
> contribution to development – their own development and that of

their communities, their countries and the world. Human security is a critical ingredient of participatory development. (Ibid.: 24)

Despite the criticisms and debates generated by academic commentators regarding the ambiguities of the concept of human security, its lack of operability, or its potential as a guide to policy-making, it could be argued that there is a great deal of conceptual clarity involved, which enables us to demarcate human security quite clearly in terms of the security discourses of resilience. First, the discourse of resilience always operates preventively, never reactively or in the post hoc manner of liberal international intervention. Secondly, the subject of human security practices is always the vulnerable subject in need of enabling agency to become resilient; never the victim, in need of external securing agency for protection. Thirdly, the inculcation of resilience is a necessity, never an option, because the starting assumption is the lack of capacity of the subject to secure itself in the future unless its securing agency is empowered.

TABLE 6.1 From Western-centred to human centred approaches to security: two paradigms

Western-centred	Human-centred
Humanitarian intervention	Human security
Protection	Resilience
1990s discourse	2000s discourse
Liberal	Neoliberal/post-liberal[1]
Intervention	Prevention/post-intervention
Rights/law	Capabilities/capacities
Post-crisis	Pre-crisis
Victims	Vulnerable
Coercive	Empowering (military force included)
Consequences addressed	Causes addressed
Direct provision/responsibility	Indirect provision/responsibility
External agency	Internal agency
Top-down	Bottom-up
Sovereign power	Dispersal of power
Western responsibility	Western facilitation
State sovereignty undermined	State sovereignty strengthened
End point exit/status quo ante	Ongoing process/open-ended

Resilience and prevention A consistent dominant thematic of the human security discourse has been that of prevention, rather than post hoc intervention:

> In recent years, responses to conflict prevention have increasingly focused on tackling the *root causes* of conflicts. This awareness has resulted in the integration of conflict *prevention* strategies into national development and poverty reduction plans. The international community has also learned that protection and *empowerment* measures are not only strategies to be adopted during and after conflicts but are also important conflict *prevention* mechanisms. As a result, protection efforts have targeted the most *vulnerable* groups, including women, children and the displaced, and have placed increasing emphasis on supporting the *capacities* of national authorities to, inter alia, provide public safety, deliver essential basic services and strengthen the rule of law. Since conflicts erode trust among communities, protection strategies are most effective when they are complemented with *empowerment* measures that promote partnerships with local and national stake-holders. Local partners can play a significant role in reinforcing *national ownership* in the country's future, nurturing reconciliation and coexistence and restoring trust in the institutions that return stability to post-conflict situations. (UNSG 2010: §51, emphases added)

As can be seen in the above paragraph, taken from the UN secretary-general's *Human Security* report to the General Assembly in April 2010, the emphasis is not upon the agency of external interveners; the problematic of human-centred approaches is that of the vulnerable. Through working on the root causes of conflict, through preventive intervention, the relationship between intervention and sovereignty is transformed. In rearticulating intervention in the language of prevention, human security reveals its conceptual distance from 1990s articulations of individual rights-centred interventions, which tended to counterpose sovereignty to international activity to promote human rights protections. International intervention is not conceived here as undermining of sovereignty but, in fact, as its precondition; the weak or failing state is held to require empowering and, thereby, the 'enhancement' of its sovereignty:

The advancement of human security requires strong and stable institutions. Among these, Governments retain the primary role in providing a rules-based system where societal relations are mutually supportive, harmonious and accountable. In cases where Government institutions are weak or under threat, the human security concept advocates addressing the root causes of these weaknesses and helps develop timely, targeted and effective responses that *improve the resilience* of Governments and people alike … the human security concept seeks to *enhance the sovereignty of States* by focusing on the multidimensional aspects of human and therefore national insecurities. Improved *capacities* of Governments and their institutions to provide early warning, identify root causes and address policy gaps in order to tackle persistent and emerging challenges are key components in advancing human security and maintaining a viable framework for promoting peace and stability. (Ibid.: §20–2, emphases added)

In this human-centred framing, sovereignty and intervention no longer stand as conceptual opposites. Early or preventive intervention, as opposed to post hoc or reactive intervention, is here understood as building or strengthening sovereignty rather than as undermining it. There is no longer a discourse which distinguishes the state as a problem requiring the limiting or constricting of sovereignty in order for external agency to secure its citizens. Here, both the post-colonial/post-conflict state and its society are seen to require enhanced capabilities in order to be able to secure themselves – to require the inculcation of resilience.

Vulnerability and empowerment The framework of human security is presented as a radical democratization of security, where the threats to human security are seen as those which threaten the security of the most vulnerable, who therefore need the most external intervention in order to enhance their capacities for security. The discourse of human security inverts a liberal understanding of sovereign securing power. The emphasis is no longer upon the sovereign acting as a securing agent; instead the emphasis must be upon a 'bottom-up' understanding of security. Securing agency is 'deliberalized' in this discourse. This is a far cry from the social contract framing of liberal modernity with the collective constitution of securing agency at the level of the state, tasking the sovereign with the post hoc duty of intervention to correct any problematic outcomes of the free interplay of market forces or of democratic contestation. Human security works in reverse. Rather than securing power being transferred to the sovereign, this securing power is decentralized or dispersed back into society (UNDP 1994: 33):

> An actor-oriented, agency-based resilience framework … reframes resilience from a systems-oriented to a people-centred perspective. It starts by considering social actors and their agency, arenas and respective agendas in the transformation of livelihoods in a resilient way. The framework proposes a normative context of entitlements, capabilities, freedoms and choices or, even more broadly, of justice, fairness and equity. An agency-based framework measures resilience in terms of how peoples' livelihood vulnerability can be reduced or, to put it more broadly, in terms of their human security. Mechanisms for *resilience-building*, from this perspective, are first and foremost about *empowering the most vulnerable* to pursue livelihood options that strengthen what they themselves consider to be their social sources of resilience. (Bohle et al. 2009: 12, emphases added)

In this dispersal of securing power, the task of the state is to focus on empowering those held to be least able to secure themselves – least able to govern themselves through reason and respond preventively to security threats. In this way, no conceptual distinction is made between the empowering practices of the domestic state and of international interveners as both are constructed as pursuing the same tasks of dispersing the power to secure, rather than as acting as securing actors per se.

In this framing, the problem of failed and failing states is precisely that they are difficult subjects for external resilience practices; that their alleged lack of capacity prevents the easy inculcation of resilience. The good governance practices that are held to assist in securing society in the liberal West are perceived to be problematic in the post-colonial world. The problematic of the inculcation of resilience has been at the centre of academic discourses. From Nobel Prize–winning development theorists, such as Amartya Sen and Douglass North, to leading security theorists, such as Paul Collier, the problem of security has been seen to be that of the difficulty of the transfer of good governance frameworks of conflict resolution and social and economic development (Sen 1999; North 1990, 2005; Collier and Hoeffler 2004; Collier et al. 2006). Once resilience is associated with good governance practices of states as the facilitators of agency, the discourses of empowerment and capability-building form the central problematic faced by human security practitioners. Good governance cannot be transferred by experts or given to fragile or conflict-prone states; good governance and resilience then become products of a process of empowering practices.

Empowerment is therefore at the centre of the problematic of human-centred approaches. In the agent-centred framework, the West no longer has the responsibility to secure, to democratize or to develop the non-Western world. This is always the lesson learned from experiences of 1990s-style interventions and their corollary of the formalized external processes of international state-building, where responsibility was directly assumed by international actors. It is for these reasons that human security can easily mesh with the concerns of 'post-liberal' approaches to peace-building, where the emphasis is squarely placed upon 'the capacity of people to decide their own future' (Martin and Owen 2010: 223; see also Richmond 2011). The regulatory mechanisms of empowerment, prevention and capacity-building are premised upon the understanding that there can be no clash of rights between sovereignty and intervention: no inside and no outside. Responsibility once again stops at the boundaries of the sovereign state, but this is a state understood as incapable of managing its autonomy without the help of external facilitators.

Conclusion

Human security framings, which seek to place the agency of the non-Western subject at the centre of security practices, have become dominant in security discourses, and have even captured or reinterpreted discourses which were originally articulated in terms of the assertion of Western responsibility. This does not mean that there is necessarily any less emphasis on military intervention; it does mean, however, that even when military intervention takes place it is discursively framed as an act of facilitating, empowering or capacity-building the vulnerable subjects on the ground. The bombing of Libya stands as a prime example of the shifting content of discourses of humanitarian intervention and the Responsibility to Protect. These concepts, at their inception, operated within liberal internationalist discourses, which posed intervention as the projection of Western securing agency through the undermining of sovereignty. Today, it is clear that they have been reinserted in a human-centred discourse – in a human security framing of empowering the Libyan state and people as agents of their own security.

Since the 1990s, the trend has been that of a shift from Western responsibility for securing the other to enabling the other to secure itself; this shift cannot be readily understood through the academic and policy analysis which understands the R2P as undermining the radical potential of human security. Rather, it seems clear that the radical framings of human security have facilitated interventionist practices, up to and including coercive military engagement. The crisis of liberal interventionism, clear in the undermining of the authority and standing of the UN at the end of the 1990s and fears over the future of international law, seems to have been resolved through the reinsertion of Western policy concerns within the human security paradigm of resilience and the agency of the vulnerable. Once this paradigm is clearly conceptually drawn out, it may be possible to understand human security frameworks not as marginal and definitely not as alternatives to the use of military force but, in fact, as dominating the international agenda and rescuing the credibility of military campaigns through evading and ameliorating the problems of legal accountability, moral legitimacy and political responsibility.

7 | CONCLUSION: REASSERTING HUMAN FREEDOM

Introduction

Human-centred discourses understand the problem of the human as the product of attempts to rise beyond our socially, biologically or ecologically imposed conditions of embeddedness. These discourses all concern the behaviour of the human subject and seek to mould this behaviour in ways that can resolve the problems we are confronted with in the world. In these approaches, the world is the starting point for seeking to reform the human. From these assumptions, the one thing excluded is the human as transformative subject. Human-centred understandings problematize the independent, goal-oriented, transformative aspects of the human. The assumption that freedom consists of the pursuit of self-determined (rather than externally determined) goals is regarded as the hubristic cause of many of the problems in the world. In taming this aspect – in problematizing the subjectivity of the human subject – the human is continually being reduced to the product of its societal environment and, at the same time and in the same process, the political is reduced to the social. The political sphere is then no longer conceived as separate or autonomous from the constraining processes of the social. For human-centred understandings, social transformation requires the self-transformation of the subject; a task in which the state (along with other governance agencies) plays the indirect role of empowering or capacity-building but never one in which it can be understood as controlling, managing or directing.

It will be argued here that, in the project of recovering the human as a political subject, Kant and Arendt are useful sources of inspiration. Distinct from dominant human-centred approaches, they encourage us to remake the world rather than to remake the human. However, the precondition for remaking the world is that humans aspire to social and political progress and act as humanly as they can in terms of struggling to build human collective institutions of meaning and action. Building or socially constructing the human scaffolding of laws and structures (as discussed in Chapter 2) enables us to act as fully as subjects in the external world as is humanly possible. Rather than demonstrating the problem of the human, through holding up the world as a mirror, Kant and Arendt suggest to us, in different ways, that the problem can be understood in terms of the subjective lack of belief in the human as a collective, acting, rational and creative subject. This concluding chapter argues for the necessity of the transformative human subject in order to critique the agent-centred concerns of ethical reflectivity, resilience, adaptation and external limits.

This chapter suggests that today's human- or agent-centred consensus derives not from globalization as a reified or external given but from the attenuation of political contestation and the concomitant weakening of the man-made structures of collective organization and meaning, which gave institutional shape to our creative engagement with the world. With the weakening of these institutional frameworks, we confront the world as alien and unknowable, as complex and globalized. We comfort ourselves that we cannot know and cannot act in the external world and turn inwards, away from the world, searching for answers not in the world but in the mystery of the human: not in our creative actions but in tracing back our behaviour and our thought processes.

In this human-centred world, ethical understandings start from the position of the world as it appears rather than from the perspective of human collectivities with goals oriented to transforming the external world. As Alain Badiou noted, this orientation reflects an ethics that 'designates above all the incapacity … to name and strive for a Good' (2001: 30). Necessity is welcomed as an ethical imperative that allows us to feel at ease with a world in which human freedom appears to be responsible for the disastrous nature of the world. In this way, ethics and necessity displace the space of politics. As Hannah Arendt explained, the appearance of necessity always involves working backwards from the status quo, whereas working forwards with a future-based orientation (acts of will) depends on the collective social and political frameworks of human meaning and organization that can enable us to cope with contingency:

> … the Will's impotence persuades men to prefer looking backward, remembering and thinking, because, to the backward glance, everything that is *appears* necessary. The repudiation of willing liberates man from a responsibility that would be unbearable if nothing that was done could be undone. (1978: II, 168)

In this world turned inwards, we no longer see ourselves as creative and constructive subjects – as humans – but as thinking subjects ill adapted to the complex societal and environmental processes through which we construct our lives and meanings. The turning of freedom into necessity, of the human-centred world, drives always to divest us of the traces of our human hubris, our meta-narratives, our teleologies and our linear thinking. We live in the world of the embedded post-liberal subject: the subject whose thoughts and behaviour need to be sensitized and adapted to the causes of peace, civility and sustainability. It thereby appears that there is only one task remaining to governments: the administrative inculcation of resilience through good governance, the environmental- or choice-framing, which will enable both individuals and societies to adapt to a world which is alien and inhospitable to us.

The following sections highlight the everyday consensus behind the imposition of human- or agent-centred approaches, extending this analysis to illustrate how even the most basic concepts of political modernity have been inverted and turned into frameworks of necessity rather than freedom. Next, this chapter considers the limits of the radical approach, despite the valuable critical insights of Foucault and Nietzsche, to suggest that, imbued with a critique of liberal modernity, these radical stances do not enable us to do more than reinscribe agent-centred understandings with a radical or critical potential. The following sections suggest that if we reject radical individualism or the deconstruction of all truth/power relations as grounds for the critique of post-liberalism (rather than its critical reaffirmation), then we may well need to return to the Enlightenment problematic of the subject. Following Kant, and emphasizing the collective rather than the individual nature of the human subject, as suggested by Arendt, it is argued here that a new philosophical construction of the political subject is necessary. In stressing the collectivity of the subject, rather than individual choices and decision-making, it may thereby be possible to re-enable a political critique for the post-liberal age.

Moralism

Human-centred understandings of the world do not provide a political programme of government. In this sense they cannot be properly understood as political. They are ethical projects in that the goal is work on the 'soul' or on the inner cognitive frameworks and capacities of the subject. In international relations theorizing, this work on the problematic subject has been central to discursive framings since the rejection of the rationalist realpolitik of the Cold War. In the 1990s, the driver behind constructivist and cosmopolitan discourses of the global was the critique of the constrained subjectivity of the masses, understood to be trapped inside the politics of the nation-state. For critical theorists, such as Andrew Linklater, the demand for cosmopolitan thinking was less about those on the other side of the world than about radicalizing the subjectivity of those closer to home, through 'expanding the realm of dialogic commitments' (1998: 109). In this way, global civil society thinking was more about a subjective ethos than about founding or supporting a political movement. It was an assertion of an ethical self-reflectivity, which was understood to be necessary to ground a radical and emancipatory politics after the defeat of movements of the left. The end of transformative politics focused on state power could result only in transformative projects focused on the human itself. Ironically, in the 2010s this same ethos is at work in the politics of post-human international relations, which similarly seeks to expand our 'dialogic commitments' beyond humanity to the other 'earthlings' with which we share our planet (Cudworth and Hobden 2011: 188) and in the new materialism which argues that in rethinking our relationship to the external world we can 'take a step toward a more ecological sensibility' (Bennett 2010a: 10).

In the inculcation of ethical self-reflectivity and resilience there is no self-determined or politically derived project or set of goals established through the public sphere of representation. The sphere of human freedom – of self-direction – no longer frames the discussion of governmental rule and its limits. The rule of necessity is post-political and post-liberal (as considered in the chapters above) and therefore radically calls into question the categories of political theory and the meaning of politics itself. It is cohered through its moral ethos of inclusion, humility and regard for the other – through its effacement of rational, subject-based, understandings of the human. In this regard, today's framings of human-centred necessity provide a secular moral certainty that argues that the 'meta-narratives' of the Enlightenment or of liberal modernity were merely products of subjective phenomenology. We feel morally at ease with the rejection of our former hubristic belief in man's reason and in man's capacity for progress. We no longer seek to impose order and meaning on the world. We are increasingly aware that, in a world of complexity, multiplicity and contingency, the attempt to impose order and reason on fluid assemblages can end only in the barbarism of liberalism, with its oppressions, exclusions and genocides, in the name of grand totalizing teleologies.

Today's human-centred morality argues (as we have seen in the opening chapters) that in a humanized world, where there is no outside, we have made or 'manufactured' our risks and our uncertainties. In other words, that it was our sciences of nature and our technology which led to the end of an external 'nature': that in 'humanizing' nature we have proved the falsity of the phenomenology of 'enlightenment', of 'science' and of 'progress'. We now know that there is no structure outside our own social and subjective creations. We have made our own world and in doing so we have discovered that we as humans no longer exist as separate from our environment and our eco-social systems.

Human- and agent-centred morality argues that in such a world we need to work on the one area that is open to human sciences – the understanding of our own behaviour and thought processes. Rather than adapting the external world to our needs and desires, we are told that we need to learn to adapt our needs and desires: to be more 'other-oriented', whether this concerns other people or the external environment. This moral ethos argues that if our problematic nature and problematic understandings and actions are revealed to us in the world we have created, then we need to pay more attention to, and to learn from, that world. We need to adapt to the world, not attempt to transform the world to meet our perceived needs (Giddens 1994; Walker and Salt 2006; Bennett 2010a).

This morality is at the centre of dominant discourses of political power. It increasingly forms the governing rationality of states across the world and of international institutions (Joseph 2012). It asserts that states can no longer act as subjects in the world, but only do their best to govern so that their own citizens and others have more capacities to reflect on and transform their own actions and behaviours. States can no longer direct, control or directly manage their societies: the world is too diverse, too complex and too contingent for this. States can only administer the frameworks in which citizens make choices and decisions for themselves. States no longer play a political role: i.e. they can no longer act as collective political representatives of society. States play a social role of enabling or empowering their societies. Any state which is unaware of, or goes against, this dominant morality, in order to pursue self-determined or autonomous ends, is seen to be lacking the sensibilities necessary to cope with our complex and globalized world and to be a potential risk to its own citizens and other states.

Legacies of politics

We should not underestimate the extent to which the moral ethos of our human-centred world has overturned the traditional conceptions of political modernity. Below, this is illustrated with a brief consideration of how a few of the key concepts of political understanding have become transformed under the human-centred gaze.

Sovereignty Sovereignty, in this framing, no longer refers to a political and legal right to self-government. This classical understanding is now seen as a merely formal, *de jure*, empty if not dangerous category. The former understanding of sovereignty, with its universalist and rationalist legacy, is understood to be particularly problematic in its silence towards the embedded nature of the subject and, with this, the illusionary nature of autonomy. Sovereignty has now become socialized; it refers to social capacities and capabilities for good governance. We have 'unbundled' sovereignty – taking out the old-fashioned and problematic idea of 'autonomy' sovereignty (Krasner 2004, 2005). We intervene today, through our human-centred policy framings, to build sovereignty as a social capacity; to fill the 'sovereignty gap' between de facto and *de jure* sovereignty (Ghani and Lockhart 2008; Ghani et al. 2005). As considered in the previous chapter, the international community intervenes to build the sovereignty-cum-social-capacity of non-Western, post-colonial or post-conflict states. This international policy intervention, into what is now considered to be a dangerous sphere of autonomy, is understood to be driven by a policy necessity that is beyond the narrow debates of national interest or of duties of cosmopolitan care.

Democracy Democracy no longer refers to the freedoms of citizens engaged in the public sphere of debate and contestation over policy goals. Democracy and the spreading of democracy are oriented around social capacities and capabilities. One thing that it seems we all can agree on today is that democracy has little to do with elections and party politics. The promotion and extension of democracy always seems to concern its shift to the social sphere, to the 'everyday' of our domestic social arrangements, or to the global sphere, discursively framed as a social, rather than political, space (for example, in terms of 'global civil society'). Governments now state that they wish to give us more democracy, by which they mean an equalizing of social power: equalizing our capacities to behave and act as 'active' or 'responsible' citizens. Foucault exactly pinpointed the intellectual roots of this possibility in the 'Platonic reversal', separating democracy from reason, and the 'Aristotelian hesitation', whereby democracy shifted from the equality of the political sphere to a matter of the sharing and equalizing of power; leading to the modern discourses of transparency and the role of civil society (2010: 184). In the human-centred world, democracy is not about reason and the exercise of power, but the opposite: with the problematizing of self-determined goals and conceptions of collective will, democracy no longer legitimizes power but serves merely as a negative or limiting factor, serving to diversify and disperse governance within society (Graham 2002). This democratizing of the social sphere in the inculcation of social capacities is understood as driven by policy necessity: the dangers of autonomy necessitate intervention in the construction of citizens, whether the problems to be addressed are those of security, development or social stability.

(Em)power(ment) The shifting understandings of sovereignty and democracy and the relocation of their focus to the social sphere of capacities and capabilities, rather than that of formal legal and political rights, highlight the transformation from discourses of freedom to those of necessity. This shift is probably most clearly articulated in the rise of discourses of empowerment. Before the shift to human-centred frameworks, controlling state power was the goal of political engagement, as without policy-making authority, changing the external world was impossible. Today political power or control over the levers of state power is not always understood to be the goal of political engagement. Many radical activists and critical commentators – from those who support the 'Occupy' movements to global civil society activists – suggest that taking state power would be a trap rather than transformative. In an agent- rather than state-centred world, often the demand is not for power but empowerment.

Agent-centred approaches reverse the relation between states and citizens. Under the liberal frameworks of modernity, citizens constituted the power of the state as the collective representative of society; now we are much more likely to understand states as giving citizens power, as the social realm subsumes the political. Under the ethos of post-liberalism, states govern through society, not over it (Foucault 2008). The axis of intervention – where government meets society – is more often the behaviour and decisions of the individual. Policy interventions then become technical questions of how the state is able to act to ethically influence citizen choices through discourses of democratization, empowerment, awareness and self-reflectivity. Internationally, conflicts and crises are held to be resolvable or preventable through social empowerment, enabling responsive adaptation and ethically aware choice-making, just as, domestically, increasing the self-reflectivity of citizens is seen to be the solution with regard to problems of pensions, welfare, health, parenting, recycling, savings, educational choices, etc. (John et al. 2011; Saint-Paul 2011). As we have seen, in this framework, the state cannot direct citizen choices but merely act to educate, empower and include; to inculcate the values of citizenship as adaptive resilience and as social capability.

Real truths

The implosion of politics – its subsumption into the social and the dominance of the morality of human-centred approaches – is a material reality. Post-liberalism has a truth, which is the existence of agent-centred frameworks of understanding across the social sciences – social constructivism, new institutionalism, organizational theory, new economics, resilience thinking, non-linear understandings, etc. It has a truth, which is the policy practices of international and domestic politics, armed with the goal of the equalizing of power, of capacity-building and social empowerment. Human-centred approaches are therefore not falsehoods. As Foucault suggested, they are not an ideological distortion imposed on the knowing subject from outside. Post-liberalism is not somehow a conscious choice of power, in order to characterize us as compliant and adaptive subjects. Agent-centred understandings tell us the truth of a world in which the human is no longer considered separate as a subject, confronting a world which is its object.

It could be argued that Foucault told us the truth of agent-centred understandings and the shift to the social before anyone else (although Arendt could be a competitor here).[1] What Foucault cannot enable (although later it will be suggested that Arendt may be able to) is the positing of an alternative truth to that of the post-liberal one. In fact, Foucault seemed relatively at ease with the truths of human-centred framings, which posed the world as complex, chaotic and non-amenable to human reason or human dominion. For the truth of post-liberalism is that there is no truth: that humanity and nature are intertwined; that politics, economics and social science are self-constituting, socially constructed disciplines, constructing and disciplining the human subject.

For Foucault, without metaphysics – without the attribution of reason to the world, initially in the figure of God – the universalizing reason-making faculties of the human could not have been given form. He sought thereby to follow Nietzsche in arguing that the death of God heralded the death of his secular replacement – the modernist teleologies of human progress. Foucault argued that in an arbitrary and chaotic world, where all human knowledge is necessarily an act of violence and power, 'then it is not God that disappears but the subject in its unity and sovereignty' (2000a: 10). In *The Order of Things*, Foucault described the 'death' or the 'unmaking' of man in the human sciences with amazing prescience, as he outlined the stakes involved in the truth of an agent-centred world:

> the double articulation of the history of individuals upon the
> unconsciousness of culture, and of the historicity of those cultures
> upon the unconscious of individuals, has opened up, without
> doubt, the most general problems that can be posed with regard to
> man. (2002: 414)

In the world become post-liberal, we understand that individuals construct their worlds often irrationally, without reason, or at least without intention. Where there were once structures of social relations, which constituted an outside to be known and transformed, now there is only the non-rational imagination of an outside (it is non-rational because we are no longer fully conscious of our cultural social constructions, which now constitute and bound our rationalities). We create our understandings of ourselves and our relationships to an outside as we create ourselves in a set of culturalized social processes, which reproduce our differences as bounded rationalities, which we can never fully comprehend as we can never fully consciously reflect on our own civilizational boundedness (Berger and Luckmann 1979).

The human-centred understanding can never work forward – assuming humans as subjects or as a collective historical subject which could give and be given meaning through liberal teleologies of knowledge and progress. The truth of post-liberalism can only ever work backwards: the nature of our problematic choice-making can only ever be known *post factum* in the world as it appears. Once the processes in which human decision-making is embedded become complex and opaque to us (as discussed earlier), we can start only from the world and never from the aspirations of the human as a goal-determining subject. We then attempt to understand the causes of the problematic choices of the individuals and societies through the process of working backwards: unearthing the path-dependent structures and intersubjective constraints upon individual and cultural understandings. It is in this attempt to understand the 'root causes' of the problems of the world in the human that politics begins to link with the 'advances' of the human sciences, driven by the policy-making attention to the inner workings of the human mind. As Foucault presciently wrote, it is in these sciences of the human that 'we see the destiny of man being spun before our eyes, but being spun backwards; it is being led back, by some strange bobbins, to the forms of its birth, to the homeland that made it possible' (2002: 416).

Before the world was post-liberal, Nietzsche had already argued the possibility that the human-centred truth of man's 'extravagant error of human conceit and irrationality' – of man as sovereign subject with the world as object – could be revealed:

> The whole attitude of 'man *versus* the world', man as world-denying principle, man as the standard of the value of things, as judge of the world, who in the end puts existence itself on his scales and finds it too light – the monstrous impertinence of this attitude has dawned upon us as such, and has disgusted us – we now laugh when we find, 'Man and World' placed beside one another, separated by the sublime presumption of the little word 'and'! (2006: 160)

We could laugh and take satisfaction, along with today's Foucauldians (if not necessarily with Foucault), over the human hubris of constituting truths or knowledge of the world and, of course, use

Nietzsche's work to do this (for Nietzsche, only the weak, who lacked the freedom of will to be self-determining, needed faith or belief in metaphysical truths). However, Nietzsche did at least flag up (merely to dismiss) the 'terrible alternative' that beckoned, as the passage quoted above continues:

> But how is it? Have we not in our very laughing just made a further step in despising mankind? And consequently also in Pessimism, in despising the existence cognisable by *us*? Have we not just thereby awakened suspicion that there is an opposition between the world in which we have hitherto been at home with our venerations – for the sake of which we perhaps *endure* life – and another world which we ourselves are: an inexorable, radical, most profound suspicion concerning ourselves ... and could easily face the coming generations with the terrible alternative: Either do away with your venerations, or – *with yourselves*! The latter would be Nihilism – but would not the former also be Nihilism? That is *our* note of interrogation. (Ibid.: 160)

For Nietzsche, the problem was the metaphysical faith in human perfection and the teleological assumptions of liberal progress. His alternative was the radical unknowability of chaos and complexity, freeing the subject from its constraints. In Nietzsche, we can already see the 'return to agency' and the abolition of structures, which are the moral truths of post-liberalism. In his assumption of the freeing of the radical self-governing, self-determining individual, he suggested that the agent-centred approach (underlying the work of critical thinkers and policy analysts today) was not necessarily nihilistic but, in fact, could be emancipatory.

From today's vantage point, in a world of chaos and complexity – which we now welcome as 'globalization' – it seems that Nietzsche's concern with nihilism – of the 'doing away' with the human itself – has been confirmed. What could be more nihilistic than the truths of the freedom-turned-into-necessity of post-liberalism? *Contra* Nietzsche, post-liberalism is nihilistic. The truth of the deconstruction of all truths does not set us free.[2] Perhaps this is why Foucault broke with Nietzsche's radical individualism to argue that we cannot escape relations of power and truth, merely attempt the 'ethos' of critique by trying to disarm the power of truth: the constructions through which truth operates to reinforce the existing hegemonies of power (2000b: 131–3).

Our morals: practical truths

While Foucault argued that we should disarm the power of all truths, which can merely act in the service of power, he did not suggest that we counter the truths of power with those of our own. I want to suggest that this is precisely what we need to do. However, I do not suggest we have a naive approach to the truth but rather that we develop a practical political approach. I think that it is in the work of Immanuel Kant that we find indications of what this approach to the possibility of truth would entail. If post-liberal and human-centred understandings rely on the impossibility of truth, then truth is necessary to step outside this problematic and to forge a political critique of post-liberalism through a struggle to reassert the transformative potential of the human subject.

Can the human still be a subject in the world? How might it be possible to argue for the possibility of human freedom through the transformation of our external world? How could we re-establish the need for a collectively constituted sphere of political equality and liberty, necessary for the pursuit of shared, collective goals? Following Kant, we cannot assert as empirical fact anything that exists in the conceptual world of philosophy, politics and political theory. The necessary idea that humans are rational subjects confronting an external world amenable to human control and dominion is not a fact: 'It is in fact merely an idea of reason, which nonetheless has undoubted practical reality' (Kant 1970: 79). For Kant there was, for example, no original social contract, in which individuals in a state of nature constituted a sovereign; however, as political subjects we nevertheless need to act as if this act had occurred: 'it is the Idea of that act that alone enables us to conceive of the legitimacy of the state' (1999: 146). It is an act of a priori reasoning which allows us to posit the Idea of the political subject: the universal rational subject.[3]

The fundamental point is that if we live in a human-centred world, we cannot merely assert the empirical existence or future existence of the transformative human subject. It seems entirely possible that following the historical defeat of the social and political struggles that gave content and meaning to the Enlightenment project, neither the empirical growth of organized labour (such as that taking place in China today) nor the coming into power of leftist governments (for example, those voted into power in Latin American states in the 2000s) can be expected to reproduce previous subjective understandings or claims with regard to the human subject. It seems that, at present, it is not possible to empirically indicate an alternative political force with programmatic aspirations reasserting the transformative political power of the subject. We do not live in the world of Karl Marx, with a coming into being of a revolutionary subject – with the promise of giving what, for the Enlightenment, was a philosophical set of a priori ideas, a practical, material and transformative reality.[4]

Today, therefore, we do not appear to live in a 'Marxist' world, we seem to live in a 'Kantian' one. We face the problems that Kant faced, of deriving the human subject, *qua* subject, from the philosophical idea rather than the concrete and material reality. We need a philosophical conception of the human as a political subject in order to keep alive even the possibility of critique. The possibility of the return of the human as a real political subject in the world is not something that can be purely addressed as an academic or philosophical question, but is one of practical politics. However, the critique of human-centred approaches seems a fundamental requirement for this return. Without an existing political movement stressing the transformative and creative possibilities of the human subject, all that remains is a moral critique, based on practical political reasoning: on the positing of the necessary idea of the human subject.

In this world, as Kant argued: 'experience cannot provide knowledge of what is right' (1970: 86). It is only through starting with a set of a priori assumptions, which assume the possibility of the existence of the human subject, that political critique can be possible. In Kant's own day, his view of the possibilities for human reasoning and progress were roundly critiqued on the basis of the chaotic, irrational and conflict-filled empirical world around us. Kant argued that his perspective was based not upon empirical fact or the truths of the world as it existed but upon his

> inborn duty of influencing posterity in such a way that it will make constant progress (and I must thus assume that progress is possible), and that this duty may be rightfully handed down from one member of the species to the next ... And however uncertain I may be and may remain as to whether we can hope for anything better for mankind, this uncertainty cannot detract from the maxim I have adopted, or from the necessity of assuming for practical purposes that human progress is possible ... It is quite irrelevant

whether any empirical evidence suggests that these plans, which are founded only on hope, may be unsuccessful. (Ibid.: 88–9)

For Kant, we had to act as human subjects with an a priori set of assumptions of what that would mean, in order to construct ourselves as humans in reality. This is why Kant held fast to the teleology of human progress, suggesting that this 'truth' did not depend on the actions or even the beliefs of individuals in the present. Today, of course, teleological assumptions of the inevitability of human progress – the metaphysical assumptions of Enlightenment idealism – can only be empty assertions, more likely to encourage fatalism than critical thinking.[5] The philosophical assumptions we need are those which ground the possibility of the universal rational subject in the present. This subject is the basis of modern frameworks of legal and political equality and, if we are to take the side of freedom rather than necessity, we need to behave as if this subject existed, even if, like the social contract, it may not have literally existed as an empirical fact. The universal rational subject may not make much sense from the scientific or socio-biological perspective, but it is not a product of nature but an artifice, a social construction, of man.[6]

All social constructions can be born and can die and the modern construction of the human is no different.[7] The modern universal construction of the rational subject has been subject to critique since the birth of the Enlightenment itself. Human-centred understandings are often posed as being the products of new developments in the external world (of globalized capitalism, complexity, technology and interdependency) or of developments in the human sciences (of neurobiology, psychology, etc.) or of the 'lessons learned' from policy failure (from the Nazi period, from the 1990s era of humanitarian intervention, from the failure of top-down institutionalist approaches to sustainable peace, etc.). In reality, however, there is little new in how agent-centred framings understand the world; what is new is the fact that these approaches can now provide a consensual basis for government policy-making and are mainly taken, like 'globalization', as the 'common sense' of our age.

Human- and agent-centred approaches can, in fact, be critically understood as a return to a Romantic understanding of the world, where nature, irrationality, emotion, affectivity, tradition, evolution, cultural difference and social embeddedness took centre place, rather than a universalist or rationalist understanding. This is why the theorists of the truth of the post-liberal often go under the name of 'new' institutionalism (Peters 2005; Steinmo et al. 1992; Scott 2008; Powell and DiMaggio 1991). This is the old institutionalism, of racial and cultural difference, of the limits of science and rationality, but without the overtly racialized understandings. Instead of cultures, producing and reproducing hierarchies of difference, we have endogenous processes of norm and knowledge production (see, further, Chandler 2012).

It would seem that we critique liberalism precisely for its progressive aspirations rather than for its limits to progress. In a world without a strong idea of the human subject, therefore, we may have to take a much more distanced view of the work of Marx – in fact, to become reluctant anti-Marxists. We may have to become enthusiastic anti-Foucauldians (despite the enticing power of Foucault's description of our world), precisely because Foucault's war on universal truths and the sovereign subject (radical and revealing in a liberal age) can only resign us to the reality of post-liberalism. Also we may have to become (perhaps reluctant) Kantians, in the realization that the categorical imperatives of the Idea are a model for critique without an empirical subject. Say what we like about 'the great Chinaman of Königsberg' (Nietzsche 1997: 82), he stands out as an example of how to undertake critique as an ethical project in the absence of a strong sense of the human subject.

The tasks of critique from the standpoint of the political subject pose specific questions of our time, in terms of what this act of practical reasoning would involve. What are the moral or practical truths that are essential in today's political context? I would like to suggest three, interlinked, practical truths that may be crucial for critique on the basis of the possibility of the future political subject.

The structure/agency distinction Human-centred approaches abolish the distinction between structure and agency. In freeing individuals from the 'truths' of structures, the world is reduced to human agency as a product of past human agency (Wendt 1992). Structure and agency are enfolded together as we seek to understand problematic and bounded choice-making in a world structured by previous problematic and bounded choice-making.[8] In the human-centred world, we make our own capitalism, we make our own conflicts and our own poverty. Without structures as practical political ideas we cannot begin to distance ourselves from the world and to socially construct the space in which we begin to act on it according to our self-chosen goals and aspirations. Politics cannot exist as the contestation of ideas if we have no conception of humans as agents and collective actors able to freely decide on their goals and thereupon to shape their circumstances.

In the human-centred world, structure and agency are reduced to process, in fact to endogenous or self-reproducing processes. These processes have no director and no centre of power. They are multiple and overlapping and, as process-based thinking is an approach, can be understood to operate at all levels, from the individual to peer groups, communities and states and to the global level. In a world reduced to processes, there is only agency. However, without structures this agency is no longer the conscious agency of a political subject transforming an external object. The agent-centred world removes structures and therefore can work only on the behaviour and choices of individuals, understood as producing and reproducing problematic outcomes. A precondition for critique in a world with such a diminished idea of the human subject is the upholding of the idea that it is possible to exert conscious transformative power upon the external world.

The political/social distinction Human-centred approaches dissipate the liberal formal world of law and politics, rights and freedoms, into the informal world of the inequalities of the social sphere. In order to defend the artificial sphere of autonomy and rights, perhaps we need to discursively separate the sphere of public contestation, requiring the fullest freedoms of speech and organization, from the world of social and economic inequality. Posing economic and social questions as problems of empowerment, of a lack of democracy and a lack of capacity, does not give agency to the marginalized and excluded; rather it places upon them the moral responsibility for the problems of the world.

Radical and participatory democracy suggest that our lives in the economic and social sphere become empowering; that our choice-making, our democracy, is about the informed choices we make and the information we receive as individuals in our everyday lives and relationships. In this case, our public lives, our good and active citizenship, would concern our everyday private decision-making in the social sphere. This extension of democracy to the social sphere, through the granting of 'empowerment rights', features strongly in the work of academics keen to expand the sphere of democracy from the formal sphere (for example, Held 1995). It seems that a precondition for critique without a strong sense of the subject is the idea of a distinction between the political and the social: we can only equalize our social and economic power by transforming the external world, not through transforming ourselves.

The world/human distinction For human-centred approaches there is no such thing as a shared or universal reality outside the inter-subjective contexts of our consciousness. In this world, theorizing is reduced to the study of human consciousness, based upon the individual's relationship to social consciousness. Instead of theories of human subjectivity, capable of relating consciousness to dynamics of material and scientific progress, post-liberalism poses the problems of the psycho-sciences at the centre of our analysis. Starting from the individual as actor and decision-maker, human-centred frameworks can operate only with mid-range theory or approaches attuned to the analysis of difference and complexity. These theories with no a priori assumptions can work only backwards to analyse the path dependencies, norms and knowledge gaps which can explain events after the fact. These theories are practice-based, micro-theories, relational theories, actor-based theories and knowledge distribution theories. For post-liberalism, there is not and cannot be anything beyond the world of appearances.

There can be no critique without a moral or philosophical construction of humanity as a collectivity, with universal and rational attributes. The struggle to raise the importance of practical political truths has been generally ignored by critical thinkers, especially those focused more upon the destruction of truths than the construction of them. It seems perhaps that our starting point today, if we do indeed wish to consider the possibility of politics after post-liberalism, rather than merely affirm the morality and truth of the human-centred world, is a reconsideration of our political and philosophical tradition from the standpoint of today's crisis of the political subject. This re-evaluation, as intimated above, would force us to reconsider positions which appeared to have been made redundant by radical critiques of classical liberalism.

A precondition for critique in a world with a diminished sense of the human subject is the philosophical assertion of human universality, the phenomenological construction of meaning beyond the finite life of the individual. However, rather than a metaphysical assertion of human progress or an understanding of history as a teleology, the claim for the human subject has to be informed by the materialist understanding of humanity as a collectively constituted subject. When we approach the world not from the human-centred standpoint of the consciousness of the individual – where it appears that we come into the world with understandings and discourses pre-existing us, standing externally to us as much as the sun, seas or mountains – but from the perspective of the collective historical subject, the processes through which we learn and engage and progress become clearer. It also becomes clear that progress is possible not because of the internal workings of individual consciousness but through the cultural and scientific understanding of humanity as a whole. A militant materialism necessarily focuses on the universal consciousness of humanity – but not in the metaphysical terms of Hegel's 'spirit' or Kant's 'soul' – and understands its development as a process of active and practical engagement with the world: as the product of the 'human' project (see the excellent treatment in Ilyenkov 1982).

Arendt and practical truth

Perhaps the most important modern thinker to have thought about the importance of practical political truths as the preconditions for politics in our modern age is Hannah Arendt. In a register sometimes similar to that of Foucault, Arendt provides a narrative of the rise of social or agent-centred understandings of the subject. Arendt's point is that, interpreted thus, the subject looks into the self for answers and meaning rather than seeing itself as a subject in the world. She argued that there could be no progress if humans were alienated from the world: for the search for the problems of the world in the sphere of life, in the sphere of human behaviour and decision-making, can only radically divide us from one another. For Arendt, only as political subjects could we construct a meaningful human world in which politics was possible.

Using this framework, or reading Arendt in terms of today, it is possible for human-centred approaches to be understood as a way of thinking which both internalizes and externalizes the human condition. Human-centred approaches understand the problems of plural and interactive humanity as being either an internal problem of the limited rationality of individuals or of the unknowability of the external world. Instead of living with contingency with the plural clash of wills and aspirations and the creative processes generated through this, we thereby seek to remove or to naturalize contingency. Human-centred approaches do both, asserting that contingency is a part of our external world – a product of globalization – and therefore natural, but also that the effects of contingency can be minimized through being aware of the problems of rationalist thinking and therefore continually working upon our own ethical self-reflectivity and upon that of others.

Rather than constituting the problem, or understanding contingency as a problem per se, for Arendt, human agency is the solution to the problem of coping with contingency. Contingency, as a fact of the world, can be managed through an appreciation of the human capacity for politics, for conscious intervention and organization. This is precisely where politics becomes important. By acting as rational and responsible citizens we come together to bind ourselves to each other and to collective projects of meaning, through our promises, contracts, treaties and constitutions. The sphere of politics – of self-determined goals – for Arendt was something that could not exist independently of practice:

> The space of appearance comes into being wherever men are together in the manner of speech and action, and therefore predates and precedes all formal constitution of the public realm and the various forms of government, that is, the various forms in which the public realm can be organised. Its peculiarity is that, unlike the spaces which are the work of our hands, it does not survive the actuality of the movement which brought it into being, but disappears ... with the disappearance or arrest of the activities themselves. (1998: 199)

Our ability to construct our world as a human one, one which is amenable to human understanding and intervention, is therefore contingent on our subjective constructions of political collectivity, which in turn shape our subjectivity and understanding of ourselves in relation to our external world. In this way, our human-centred understanding of the imposition of necessity over freedom is neither a trick of ideology nor a product of the external world, but rather the real, but contingent, reflection of our lack of human activity and engagement in constructing a human world. The loss of world and the internalized understanding of transformative agency are products of a broader problematic of real material political and ideological defeat of struggles to construct a human world.

Arendt suggested that in the shift to the social away from politics as a public sphere, power becomes less visible, that the connections between individuals become less clear, and that politics becomes reduced to the administration of natural or social processes. It was then inevitable that the problematic of the human – and the 'making' or 'capacity-building' or 'empowerment' of the individual – displaced externally oriented political engagement: 'This attempt to replace acting with making is manifest in the whole body of argument against "democracy", which, the more consistently and better reasoned it is, will turn into an argument against the essentials of politics' (ibid.: 220). She argued further that:

> The calamities of action all arise from the human condition of plurality, which is the condition *sine qua non* for that space of appearance which is the public realm. Hence the attempt to do away with this plurality is always tantamount to the abolition of the public realm itself. (Ibid.: 220)

Human-centred discourses can be understood as 'making' dis-courses in the sense that they attempt to manage and remove the contingencies of human existence. However, Arendt went further, to highlight the deeper problematization of the human subject itself; contingency becomes a problem because we have lost a sense of public reason and public power as a way of managing contingency. If we are unable to cope with uncertainty and contingency, the inevitable result is that:

> All this is reason enough to turn away with despair from the realm of human affairs and to hold in contempt the human capacity for freedom, which by producing the web of human relationships, seems to entangle its producer to such an extent that he appears much more the victim and the sufferer than the author and doer of what he has done. Nowhere ... does man appear to be less free than in those capacities whose very essence is freedom and in that

realm which owes its existence to nobody and nothing but man. (Ibid.: 233–4)

In a world dominated by human- and agent-centred understandings, man appears to be unfree and the presuppositions of the political and public sphere seem to be hubristic and false. Human-centred approaches reflect this disappearance of man, charted by Arendt in terms of the natural and social sciences, whereby 'man began to consider himself part and parcel of the two superhuman, all-encompassing processes of nature and history', both of which produced contingencies 'without ever reaching any inherent *telos* or approaching any pre-ordained idea' (ibid.: 307). In these framings, rather than humans as active and creative subjects, the understanding of the human becomes one of the processes in which they are embedded subjects, open to the understandings of behaviouralist and natural sciences. The solution to the problems of the world then becomes sought inside the human head and in the processes within which the human is embedded, with the serious danger 'that man may be willing and, indeed, is on the point of developing into that animal species from which, since Darwin, he imagines he has come' (ibid.: 322).

Arendt suggested that thinking in terms of the need to adapt to the external world was the opposite to the aspiration for human freedom. For her, the public sphere of the political process was precisely distinguished from the sphere of external necessity. The social sphere was that of necessity and inequality, whereas the polis was the sphere of free engagement among equals (ibid.: 32). Arendt argued that it was only in the public sphere that individuation mattered, where individuals could be distinguished by actions and deeds. In the social sphere, all that mattered was the mass, to which could be applied the sciences of economics and the methods of statistical analysis, ruling out of the picture creative individuals (ibid.: 42–3). Once the public sphere was reduced to the social and the management of society, then politics and the state gave way to 'pure administration'. We have a 'withering away of the state' as predicted by Marx, but not through the mechanism of revolution (ibid.: 45).

This 'withering away of the state' is of fundamental importance for grasping the problematic nature of human-centred approaches. The sensibilities of both Arendt and Foucault, regarding the destati-fication, socialization or biopoliticization of the state, are informed through the founding and experience of the post-war West German state. The state which was to become not the exception to liberal frameworks of rule (where both the state and its citizens needed to be desubjectified and worked upon to enable their adaptive autonomy rather than the constitution of public power and external goal-directed activity) but the exemplar for the post-modern age and the model for the European Union as an actor without sovereign subjecthood. In the human-centred state, the state is no longer separate from or above society but can work only through society. Without constituting itself as a subject, with autonomously directed goals, there is no politics, merely the addressing of problems, responding to the external world, through the administrative mechanisms of facilitation, capacity-building, empowerment and the inculcation of ethical self-reflectivity or resilience. While the work on the transformation of the self – the subsuming of the political into the social – may sound like a radical, progressive and liberating approach, we can choose to understand this (I suggest) as rule through necessity rather than (and against) a conception of rule through freedom.

Arendt presciently noted that when the social displaces the public political sphere, there is no longer personal responsibility for deeds and words (action) and people are judged according to their behaviour. She noted the development of 'the all-comprehensive pretension of the social sciences which, as "behavioural sciences", aim to reduce man as a whole, in all his activities, to the level of a conditioned and behaving animal' (ibid.: 45). Perhaps even more pertinently, she noted that: 'through society it is the life process itself which in one form or another has been channelled into the public realm' (ibid.: 45). The realm of necessity, of the natural, then predominates over the human. In this world, it seems that our sciences of the social and the political lag far behind our achievements in the natural sciences; that the human is the problem despite science and technology. Arendt argued:

> this criticism concerns only a possible change in the psychology of
> human beings – their so-called behaviour patterns – not a change
> of the world they move in. And this psychological interpretation,
> for which the absence or presence of a public realm is as irrelevant
> as any tangible, worldly reality, seems rather doubtful in view of
> the fact that no activity can become excellent if the world does not
> provide a proper space for its exercise. (Ibid.: 49)

She suggests the resurrection of the public realm as an alternative to the current insistence that politics be reduced to the administration of 'behavioural change'. The removal of the public sphere means that we live together in the world without bonds of connection. The public sphere may be a constructed and artificial world but it is one which is common to all of us, as a human construction or artifice, which brings us together as equals by virtue of separating us from our private lives and existences but at the same time makes us separate and individuated as responsible actors (ibid.: 52–3). Without a public realm, human life really is embedded in overlapping complex adaptive systems within which the human is reduced to a fleeting individual life.

The subject or problematic of politics today becomes the 'inner subjectivity of the individual', which was previously outside the realm of the public and was a private concern. Arendt saw this as 'a flight from the whole outer world' (ibid.: 69). The focus on the inner world denied what was core to the human subject in traditional political thought. In human-centred thinking, therefore, we are all subject to necessity and called upon to adapt to this. In this world there is no separation of the public from the private. As Arendt notes, for Aristotle, the slave lacked the freedom essential to the human condition, especially two essential qualities: the capacity to deliberate and decide; and the capacity to foresee and to choose. The slave was reduced to the status of a non-human or animal-like existence because the slave was subject to necessity (ibid.: 84).

Human-centred approaches talk about capacity-building the subject, but this is always in response to the problems of the external world held to be caused by this lack of capacity. Goal-directed approaches, autonomously or freely chosen, do not feature in this understanding. The creative freedoms of the subject as subject in the world, our distinctively human features, are thereby removed. For Arendt, this problematizing of the human as a creative, transformative subject rather than as an object to be transformed was reminiscent of the Socratic rejection of politics and the public sphere – a renouncing of the human capacity for 'action', in her terminology: 'It is as though they had said that if men only renounce their capacity for action, with its futility, boundlessness, and uncertainty of outcome, there could be a remedy for the frailty of human affairs' (ibid.: 195).

Conclusion

Humans make the world but not in conditions of their own choosing, as we know from Marx (1852), of course. The important point, which we glean from Kant and Arendt, is that of the contingent consequences of the choices we make in response to these conditions. We do not choose the consequences, in the sense that we can be held responsible for the outcomes. In our choices we do not produce the world, we merely provide the basis for myriads of other choices and responses and ideas, which are grounded and cohered in the collective human engagement with the materiality of the world. The world is full of opportunities for us to make new choices and to experiment with new ways of thinking and to learn and progress on the basis of new knowledge. For human-centred approaches, the problematic – the point of social intervention – is always constructed through working back from the world to adjust the choices and decisions which the individual makes. The world as it exists is always separated into discrete processes, which can be directly traced backwards to the decision of individuals, and then further backwards to the consciousness of the individual as it is shaped by experience. Governance starts from the consequences, from the world, and works backwards to unmake or remake the human as the object of intervention.

Kant and Arendt take us out of the concern with unmaking or remaking the individual as decision-maker, to the social processes and social and plural reality, which is the context in which these individual choices are made and are understood. They encourage us to view the collective human project as one that works behind the backs of individuals – a 'process without a subject', as Althusser (2008) would argue. They encourage us to remake the world rather than to remake the human. However, the precondition for remaking the world is that humans act as humanly as they can in terms of struggling to build human collective institutions of meaning and action. Rather than demonstrating the problem of the human through holding up the world as a mirror, Kant and Arendt suggest that the problem is the subjective lack of belief in the human as a collective, acting, rational and creative subject.

The human project, as a practical political truth, with a moral or philosophical grounding, has to be always an open and contingent one; always open to new problems and new situations and new solutions and new ways of thinking. The project of perfecting the human can never be inward or closed, can never reach an end or final goal, can never be judged by or derived from external circumstances or truths, because what it means to be human can only ever be known in struggle and is therefore open ended. In the world dominated by human and agent-centred understandings, the human project is assumed to be dead, a mistake, a hubristic error. Post-liberalism understands humans purely in their non-rational aspects because the creative, constructive aspects – through which reason is developed individually and collectively – are regarded as precisely those which need to be tamed. In taming this aspect, in problematizing the subjectivity of the human subject, the human is continually being reduced to the societal, biological and environmental relations in which it is embedded, in the same way that the political is reduced to the social.

With the reduction of the subject to an object or product of processes in which it is embedded, human-centred understandings necessarily problematize the human. This problematization is not based on 'freeing' human agency but on freeing the human from the illusion of rational agency and self-directed goals or aspirations. This framing necessarily reduces the political to the social realm and the inculcation of ethical self-reflectivity, reasoned autonomy or resilience. There could not be two more sharply opposed ontological standpoints than that between the classical Enlightenment understanding of the subject and today's human-centred conception of the post-liberal subject. The precondition for human progress is the taking of an affirmative moral position on the human as transformative subject rather than as the object in need of transformation.

NOTES

1 Introduction

1 The UK minister for decentralization and cities, Greg Clark, for example, argues that for 'much of the time and in many areas of policy, simply telling people what to do can be wholly counterproductive, especially at a time when deference is low and mistrust of politicians and civil servants is high' (Clark 2011: vi).

2 The transformation of the military in many European states is a good example of the erosion of traditional forms of authority, highlighted in the increasing individual responsibility of soldiers, where ethics and legal training provides and calls for individual self-reflectivity over when to obey or to disobey orders.

3 Particularly from Foucault's lectures on governmentality delivered in 1978 and 1979 (see further Dean 2010: 261).

4 Because the socialist or Marxist project involved the submerging of the state into society, rather than the liberal understanding of its suspension above the social realm of freedom, Foucault suggests that it is not possible to talk of a 'socialist governmentality' (2008: 93–4). There is therefore no post-liberal governmentality which articulates the practices and processes of government in relation to the free subject of rule, any more than, as Arendt states, we can properly speak of 'Marxist forms of government' (Arendt 2005: 90).

5 It should be noted that the ontology of human-centred understandings, starting from the complexity of the world of appearances and working backwards to reform or reshape human choice-making, displacing the goals of political activity with sensibilities and reflectivity with regard to the external world, in order to work on the transformation of the self, can also be seen to be at work in the post-human or new materialist critiques of 'anthropocentric' approaches (see, for example, Latour 1993; Bennett 2010a). The striking similarities between these frameworks casts doubt on the radical claims of agent-centred understandings, either in human or post-human guise.

2 From freedom to necessity

1 This trend is clear across the social sciences and humanities and is particularly highlighted in the growing popularity of new materialist approaches which 'distribute' agency to non-human actors and, in more radical approaches, to inanimate objects, operating within complex assemblages with their own emergent agential power (see, for example, Coole and Frost 2010a; Bennett 2010a).

2 Mahatma Gandhi is often credited with putting this point most lucidly: 'Freedom is not worth having if it does not connote freedom to err. It passes my comprehension how human beings, be they ever so experienced and able, can delight in depriving other human beings of that precious right' (Gandhi 1931).

3 In fact, it is only when human actions are understood as inserted into contingent and complex assemblages that human responsibility is diluted or distributed in ways in which it is no longer meaningful (see, for example, Bennett 2010a: 37).

4 Just as Nietzsche found solace in the idea that, although his work might not find favour among his currently available audience, future generations might appreciate his intellectual struggle, such that he would, in fact, be 'born posthumously' (2007b: 93). Nietzsche also adopted a strong understanding of the need to accept failure, mistakes or misfortune at the personal level in his famous aphorism 'That which does not kill me, makes me stronger' (2007a: 5).

5 In the pre-modern age, for example in Ancient Greece, there was an understanding of the public sphere of citizenship as one where there was freedom from the necessity of privatized toil, but this sphere of freedom always coexisted with and was dependent upon the hierarchical division of society excluding slaves and women from this sphere. It was only with the modernist promise of material transformation that universal ideas of freedom could arise.

6 The essential relation between the social construction of a law-bound external world and a human subject capable of goal-determining freedom has been highlighted in some of the more insightful new materialist analysis, aspiring to deconstruct this 'ontological dualism' for its 'specifically modern attitude or ethos of subjectivist potency' (Coole and Frost 2010b: 8; Frost 2010: 171).

7 The heightened importance of these limits was famously articulated in the run-up to the Iraq war by the former US Secretary of Defense Donald Rumsfeld (2002) as the 'unknown unknowns: the things we do not know we don't know'.

8 As Hannah Arendt repeatedly commented, this understanding of history as contingent, as beyond human responsibility, but still as a meaningful product of human actions, was conceptualized by Kant as a 'ruse of nature' or works of 'providence' and by Hegel as 'the cunning of reason' (for example, 2005: 57). The concluding chapter of this book returns to the problematic of how the metaphysical understanding of history or progress of the Enlightenment era can be replaced by a materialist analysis of contingency that puts human agency and human consciousness at the forefront.

9 I emphasize human freedom here, as we increasingly tend to use 'freedom' in ways which remove or decentre the human subject. A good example here is the work of Jane Bennett, who uses 'freedom' to describe unpredictable or undetermined outcomes, where the links between cause and effect are contingent. Here, 'freedom' is the product of the lack of a knowable and predictable world; it is, in Arendtian terms, the freedom of the desert (Bennett 2010b: 61).

3 Resilience

1 This could be understood as the major contribution of the French 'social action' sociologist Alain Touraine, whose work is unfortunately not more widely read in the English-speaking world. The subtitle of this chapter is, in fact, taken from the English translation of his 1973 book *Production de la société* (Touraine 1977).

2 As leading medical professionals dealing with resilience and child mental health, Ann Masten and Jenifer Powell, state: 'Resilience refers to patterns of positive adaptation in the context of significant risk or adversity ... Technically, to call a person resilient would be improper in diagnostic terminology because resilience is a description of a general pattern ... It might be more appropriate to say that "This person has a resilience pattern" or "This person shows the features of resilience". It is also important to keep in mind that identifying resilience from explicit

or implicit diagnostic criteria is not assumed to describe people in totality or to define their lives at all times. Hence, one would expect individuals who meet the criteria for resilience to differ in many other ways, and one would not expect a resilient person, however defined at one point in time, to be doing well every minute of the day, under all imaginable circumstances, or in perpetuity. Resilience is not a trait of an individual, though individuals manifest resilience in their behavior and life patterns.' (Masten and Powell 2003: 4)

3 The Demos Resilient Nation Advisory Group defines resilience as: 'The capacity of an individual, community or system to adapt in order to sustain an acceptable level of function, structure, and identity' (Edwards 2009: 18).

4 The contradiction between the asserted aim of 'reducing the state' and the consequences of non-legislative state interference in the private sphere is well drawn out in the written evidence to the UK government Public Administration Select Committee (Richards and Smith 2011).

5 'A spider conducts operations that resemble those of a weaver, and a bee puts to shame many an architect in the construction of her cells. But what distinguishes the worst architect from the best of bees is this, that the architect raises his structure in imagination before he erects it in reality ... He not only effects a change of form in the material on which he works, but he also realizes a purpose of his own that gives the law to his modus operandi, and to which he must subordinate his will' (Marx 1954: 174).

6 It could be argued that the dominant framings of modern social theory, from social constructivism to new institutionalism (in all its normative, historical, empirical, rational-choice, sociological and international hues),

depend on the asserted overcoming of the structure/agency divide (the fundamental Cartesian divide between the inner and outer worlds) (see, for example, Berger and Luckmann 1979; Peters 2005; Scott 2008; Steinmo et al. 1992; Mahoney and Thelen 2010).

4 Development and human agency

1 For Marx, 1830 marked the turning point, from which point onwards the science of political economy, which reached its high point with Ricardo, could only degenerate and become vulgarized: 'In France and England the bourgeoisie had conquered political power. Thenceforth, the class struggle, practically as well as theoretically, took on more and more outspoken and threatening forms. It sounded the knell of scientific bourgeois economy. It was thenceforth no longer a question, whether this theorem or that was true, but whether it was useful to capital or harmful, expedient or inexpedient, politically dangerous or not. In place of disinterested inquirers, there were hired prize-fighters; in place of genuine scientific research, the bad conscience and the evil intent of apologetic' (1954: 24–5).

2 For Marx and Engels, the idealism of the Enlightenment perspective, which Foucault so correctly highlights and deploys as the basis of his critique of neoliberalism, was perceived to have been overcome through the materialist analysis of social relations and the emergence of a universal class which needed to transform these relations in order to emancipate itself: the industrial proletariat. Of course, if this collective agent of self-transformation were not to appear or if it was to suffer a historical class defeat rather than achieve its ultimate aims, then it would appear that it was the Enlightenment which both gave

birth to and foretold the death of the 'human' as a self-realizing subject. The inability of humanity to give meaning to the world through the Enlightenment and therefore the shift to conceiving of itself and its meaning-creating subjectivity as the problem in need of resolution is, of course, acutely articulated by Nietzsche (see, in particular, 'Our note of interrogation', 2006: 159–60).

3 Here we can see clear parallels between the problematic of human-centred development and discussions of resilience, considered in the previous chapter.

4 A similar approach can be seen in the UK government's 2012 Social Justice Strategy, which sets out 'an ambitious new vision for supporting the most disadvantaged individuals and families in the UK', through focusing on prevention throughout a person's life, with carefully designed interventions. The importance of family is therefore heavily emphasized as 'the most important building block in a child's life' (HMG 2012).

5 The social construction of difference

1 A common definition of norms in the IR literature is that proposed by Peter J. Katzenstein, as a description of 'collective expectations for the proper behaviour of actors with a given identity' (Katzenstein 1996a: 5).

2 The understanding of classical liberal theory as being blind to social and associative connections has been authoritatively challenged by authors as diverse as C. B. Macpherson (1962) and Amartya Sen (see, for example, 1987, 2009).

3 I follow Wesley Widmaier (2011), although, for heuristic purposes, the analytical framing of these stages differs.

4 For more on the problematic of universalism and the overcoming of difference in the Enlightenment conception of 'free' and autonomous subjects, see the treatment by Michel Foucault (2010: 6–39). See also the insightful work of Laura Zanotti (2006, 2011).

5 Neoliberalism in international relations theory refers to theorists who worked in the same methodological tradition as realist theories but who argued that the pursuit of rational self-interest could lead to cooperation rather than conflict.

6 For example, for the sociologically informed authors of the United Nations–instigated 'Responsibility to protect' report, the domestic socio-political context or preconceived geo-political interests were no excuse for not choosing to behave according to global liberal norms: 'The behaviour of states is not predetermined by systemic or structural factors, and moral justifications are not merely after-the-fact justifications or simply irrelevant' (ICISS 2001b: 129).

7 This was reminiscent of the 'universalist' reasoning of Vitoria, regarding the Spanish conquest of the New World, where refusal to open up to *liberum commercium* and the communicative engagement of papal missionaries was held to be a violation of Spanish rights justifying suppression (Schmitt 2003: 108–13).

8 For this reason the international administrative mandate was initially intended to last only until the first elections, held in September 1996 (for more information, see Chandler 1999).

9 In shifting policy concerns to the societal rather than the state level, democratic norms discourse followed similar international discourses concerned with security and development, where the emphasis on 'human' individual and social capacities and capabilities was intellectually cohered through the work of Amartya Sen and others (as discussed in the previous chapter; see particularly Sen 1999 and the UN *Development*

Reports, annually from 2004, and, for a critique, Duffield 2007).

10 Previously, Thomas Risse-Kappen had argued that domestic institutional structures had blocking effects, in terms of preventing communicative engagement with international norm entrepreneurs or transnational non-state actors from accessing domestic political systems and domestic actors (see, for example, Risse-Kappen 1994, 1995).

11 It is in this context that concerns are often expressed in terms of the limits of the European Union's 'normative power' beyond the periphery of states involved in the accession process (see, for example, Laïdi 2008: 15).

12 There is no methodological necessity for social constructivists to argue for the globalization of liberal norms rather than focus on the barriers to their acceptance – the only difference is the level of focus for the endogenous understanding of the operation of societal intersubjective framings. Whereas earlier norms-based approaches focused on global social interaction, overtly challenging rationalist approaches at the international level, later norms-based approaches have focused on the domestic level of failing or post-conflict states and have tended to present endogenous frameworks of understanding in terms of institutionalist frameworks of reasoning, which equally challenge traditional rationalist frameworks of understanding in economic and political social science.

13 As Lord Paddy Ashdown, the former international High Representative with administrative governing responsibilities for Bosnia, explained informally to me, in January 2011, external rule was necessary only until the Bosnian people were judged to be capable of freely making their own rational governmental decisions (see also Ashdown 2007).

14 Katzenstein, Keohane and Krasner argue that: 'Constructivists seek to understand how preferences are formed and knowledge generated, prior to the exercise of instrumental rationality' (1998: 681).

15 Foucault traces the institutionalist, agent-centred turn in social theorizing back to Husserl's critique of phenomenology, which influenced the Freiburg School of neoliberal economic thinking as much as it did the critical sociologists of the Frankfurt School (2008: 101–6; see also Chandler 2010a: 66–84).

16 This danger was articulated well by Keohane, in a defence of rationalist understandings that encouraged researchers 'to look beneath the surface' rather than merely focus on 'post hoc observation of values or ideology' (Keohane 1988). Or, as Karl Marx put it: 'all science would be superfluous if the outward appearance and the essence of things directly coincided' (Marx n.d.).

6 Empowerment and human security

1 The distinction with classical liberal security discourses of intervention is drawn out in relation to neoliberal or biopolitical framings in Foucault (2008) and post-liberal framings in Chandler (2010a).

7 Conclusion

1 The recent work of Patricia Owens usefully draws out the ways in which Arendt's work can add to Foucauldian understandings of the shift to the social (Owens 2012).

2 In fact, Arendt notes that Nietzsche was the first to recognize the shift away from the world but that 'it was also Nietzsche who made the first decisive mistake in diagnosing it' (2005: 201).

3 In Chapter 4, I suggested that the voluntarism of Kant was problematic

as a framework of explanation for the reproduction of social inequalities or as a way of resolving them. However, the voluntaristic 'act of will' is essential for the initiation of a politics of resistance or for academic critique. This voluntaristic side of critique becomes increasingly mediated as critique takes an organized material or collective (rather than academic or philosophical) political form.

4 Marx's critique of Kant, nevertheless, still stands, for as long as this subject was engaged in the process of struggle, to make the world human, philosophical conceptions of the subject, idealized as a set of a priori categorical injunctions, could act only as a critique of the real process of change.

5 As Arendt noted in her Kant lectures, the problem of how to deal meaningfully with the present is evaded in Kant's resort to the metaphysics of history or progress (1982: 77).

6 The same could be said regarding even the distinction between humans and non-humans or living beings and inanimate matter. While it is possible to follow new materialist or object-based theorists in their deconstruction of these subject/object binaries (for example, Latour 1993; Coole and Frost 2010a; Harman 2010), the political consequences of such a shift are rarely fully drawn out. More worryingly, for authors like Jane Bennett, it is important to consciously 'elide the question of the human' (2010a: 120) and 'to question the question: Why are we so keen to distinguish the human self from the field?' (ibid.: 121).

7 As Foucault so presciently noted in his famous description of 'man' as a transient 'invention of recent date', which, with a shift in our understandings, 'would be erased, like a face drawn in sand at the edge of the sea' (2002: 422).

8 Even critical realists, keen to focus on frameworks of structure and agency, seem concerned less with the need for distinguishing these than on the need to emphasize the relational blurring between them (see, for example, Wight 2006).

BIBLIOGRAPHY

Acharya, A. (2000) 'How ideas spread: whose norms matter? Norm localization and institutional change in Asian regionalism', *International Organization*, 2(1): 65–87.

AJIL (1999) 'Editorial comments: NATO's Kosovo intervention', *American Journal of International Law*, 93(4): 824–62.

Alkire, S. (2004) 'A vital core that must be treated with the same gravitas as traditional security threats', *Security Dialogue*, 35(3): 359–60.

Althusser, L. (2008) 'Reply to John Lewis', in *On Ideology*, London: Verso, pp. 61–139.

Archibugi, D. (2000) 'Cosmopolitical democracy', *New Left Review*, 2(4): 137–50.

— (ed.) (2003) *Debating Cosmopolitics*, London: Verso.

Arendt, H. (1978) *The Life of the Mind*, New York: Harvest.

— (1982) *Lectures on Kant's Political Philosophy*, Brighton: Harvester Press.

— (1998) *The Human Condition*, 2nd edn, Chicago, IL: University of Chicago Press.

— (2005) *The Promise of Politics*, New York: Schocken Books.

Ashdown, P. (2007) 'The European Union and statebuilding in the Western Balkans', *Journal of Intervention and Statebuilding*, 1(1): 107–18.

Badiou, A. (2001) *Ethics: An Essay on the Understanding of Evil*, London: Verso.

Barnett, M. (2008) 'Social constructivism', in J. Baylis, S. Smith and P. Owens (eds), *The Globalization of World Politics: An Introduction to International Relations*, Oxford: Oxford University Press.

Barnett, M. and C. Zürcher (2009) 'The peacebuilder's contract: how external statebuilding reinforces weak statehood', in R. Paris and T. D. Sisk (eds), *The Dilemmas of Statebuilding: Confronting the Contradictions of Postwar Peace Operations*, London: Routledge, pp. 23–52.

Baudrillard, J. (2002) *The Spirit of Terrorism*, London: Verso.

Bellamy, A. (2009) *Responsibility to Protect: The Global Effort to End Mass Atrocities*, London: Polity.

Belloni, R. (2008) 'Civil society in war-to-democracy transitions', in A. K. Jarstad and T. D. Sisk (eds), *From War to Democracy: Dilemmas of Peacebuilding*, Cambridge: Cambridge University Press, pp. 182–210.

Ben-Ami, D. (2006) 'Who's afraid of economic growth', *Spiked*, 4 May, www.spiked-online.com/articles/0000000CB04D.htm.

Bennett, A. and A. L. George (1997) 'Process tracing in case study research', Presented at the MacArthur Foundation Workshop on Case Study Methods, 17–19 October, users.polisci.wisc.edu/kritzer/teaching/ps816/ProcessTracing.htm.

Bennett, J. (2010a) *Vibrant Matter: A Political Ecology of Things*, London: Duke University Press.

— (2010b) 'A vitalist stopover on the way to a new materialism', in D. Coole and S. Frost (eds), *New Materialisms: Ontology, Agency and Politics*, London: Duke University Press, pp. 47–69.

Berger, P. and T. Luckmann (1979) *The Social Construction of Reality: A Treatise in the Sociology of Knowledge*, London: Penguin.

Black, D. (1999) 'The long and winding road: international norms and domestic political change in South Africa', in T. Risse, S. C. Ropp and K. Sikkink (eds), *The Power of Human Rights: International Norms and Domestic Change*, Cambridge: Cambridge University Press.

Bohle, H.-G., B. Etzold and M. Keck (2009) 'Resilience as agency', *IHDP Update*, 2.2009: 8–13, www.ihdp.unu.edu/file/get/7699.

Booth, K. (1991) 'Security in anarchy: utopian realism in theory and practice', *International Affairs*, 67(3): 527–45.

Brassett, J. and N. Vaughan-Williams (2011) 'Performative ecologies of resilience and trauma: a critical analysis of UK civil contingencies', Paper presented at the Centre for Citizenship, Identities and Governance workshop 'Resisting (in) security, securing resistance', Open University, London, 12 July.

Briggs, R. (2010) 'Community engagement for counterterrorism: lessons from the United Kingdom', *International Affairs*, 86(4): 971–81.

Brown, C. (1994) '"Turtles all the way down": anti-foundationalism, critical theory and international relations', *Millennium: Journal of International Studies*, 23(2): 213–36.

Bull, H. (1977) *The Anarchical Society: A Study of Order in World Politics*, London: Macmillan.

Bulley, D. (2011) 'Producing and governing community (through) resilience', Paper presented at the 'Resilient futures: the politics of preventive security' workshop, Department of Politics and International Studies, University of Warwick, 27/28 June.

Burchell, G. (1991) 'Peculiar interests: civil society and the "system of natural liberty"', in G. Burchell, C. Gordon and P. Miller (eds), *The Foucault Effect: Studies in Governmental Rationality*, London: Harvester Wheatsheaf, pp. 119–50.

— (1996) 'Liberal government and techniques of the self', in A. Barry, T. Osbourne and N. Rose (eds), *Foucault and Political Reason: Liberalism, Neo-Liberalism and Rationalities of Government*, London: UCL Press, pp. 19–36.

Burg, S. L. (1997) 'Bosnia Herzegovina: a case of failed democratization', in K. Dawisha and B. Parrot (eds), *Politics, Power, and the Struggle for Democracy in South-East Europe*, Cambridge: Cambridge University Press, pp. 122–45.

Burgess, A. (1997) *Divided Europe: The New Domination of the East*, London: Pluto.

Buzan, B. (2004) 'A reductionist, idealistic notion that adds little analytical value', *Security Dialogue*, 35(3): 369–70.

Campbell, S., D. Chandler and M. Sabaratnam (eds) (2011) *A Liberal Peace? The Problems and Practices of Peacebuilding*, London: Zed Books.

Carothers, T. (2004) *Critical Mission: Essays on Democracy Promotion*, Carnegie Endowment for International Peace.

CGG (1995) *The Report of the Commission for Global Governance: Our Global Neighbourhood*, Oxford: Oxford University Press.

Chakrabortty, A. (2010) 'Cameron's hijacking of Nudge theory is a classic example of how big ideas get corrupted', *Guardian*, 7 December.

Chandler, D. (1998) 'Democratization in Bosnia: the limits of civil society building strategies', *Democratization*, 5(4): 78–102.

— (1999) *Bosnia: Faking Democracy after Dayton*, London: Pluto Press.

— (2001) 'Universal ethics and elite politics: the limits of normative human rights theory', *International Journal of Human Rights*, 5(4): 72–89.

— (2004) *Constructing Global Civil Society: Morality and Power in International Relations*, Basingstoke: Palgrave Macmillan.

— (2006) *Empire in Denial: The Politics of State-Building*, London: Pluto Press.

— (2008) 'Human security: the dog that didn't bark', *Security Dialogue*, 39(4): 427–38.

— (2009a) *Hollow Hegemony: Rethinking Global Politics, Power and Resistance*, London: Pluto Press.

— (2009b) 'Unravelling the paradox of "the responsibility to protect"', *Irish Studies in International Affairs*, 20: 27–39.

— (2010a) *International Statebuilding: The Rise of Post-Liberal Governance*, London: Routledge.

— (2010b) 'Race, culture and civil society: peacebuilding discourse and the understanding of difference', *Security Dialogue*, 41(4): 369–90.

— (2012) 'Promoting democratic norms? Social constructivism and the "subjective" limits to liberalism', *Democratization*, 19, forthcoming.

Chandler, D. and N. Hynek (eds) (2011) *Critical Perspectives on Human Security: Rethinking Emancipation and Power in International Relations*, London: Routledge.

Checkel, J. (1998) 'The constructivist turn in international relations theory', *World Politics*, 50(2): 324–48.

Chimni, B. (2008) 'The Sen conception of development and contemporary international law discourse: some parallels', *Law and Development Review*, 1(1).

Cilliers, P. (1998) *Complexity and Post-modernism: Understanding Complex Systems*, London: Routledge.

Clark, D. A. (2005) 'The capability approach: its development, critiques and recent advances', Working Paper 32, Global Poverty Research Group, November, www.gprg.org/pubs/workingpapers/pdfs/gprg-wps-032.pdf.

Clark, G. (2011) 'Foreword', in P. John et al., *Nudge, Nudge, Think, Think: Experimenting with Ways to Change Civic Behaviour*, London: Bloomsbury, pp. v–vi.

Clarke, J. and J. Nicholson (2010) *Resilience: Bounce Back from Whatever Life Throws at You: Practical Solutions for Taking Control and Surviving in Difficult Times*, Surrey: Crimson Publishing.

Coaffee, J., D. M. Wood and P. Rogers (2009) *The Everyday Resilience of the City: How Cities Respond to Terrorism and Disaster*, Basingstoke: Palgrave Macmillan.

Collier, P. (2010) *Wars, Guns and Votes: Democracy in Dangerous Places*, London: Vintage.

Collier, P. and A. Hoeffler (2004) 'Greed and grievance in civil war', *Oxford Economic Papers*, 56: 563–95.

Collier, P., A. Hoeffler and D. Rohner (2006) 'Beyond greed and grievance: feasibility and civil war', Centre for the Study of African Economies Working Paper Series 2006-10, 7 August.

Commission for Africa (2005) *Our Common Interest*, www.commissionforafrica.info/2005-report.

Commons, J. R. (1936) 'Institutional economics', *American Economic Review*, 26(Supplement): 237–49.

Condorcet, A.-N. (2009 [1795]) *Outlines of an Historical View of the Progress of the Human Mind*, Chicago, IL: G. Langer.

Connolly, W. (2004) 'Method, problem, faith', in I. Shapiro, R. M. Smith and

T. E. Masoud (eds), *Problems and Methods in the Study of Politics*, Cambridge: Cambridge University Press, pp. 332–9.

Coole, D. and S. Frost (2010a) *New Materialisms: Ontology, Agency and Politics*, London: Duke University Press.

— (2010b) 'Introducing the new materialisms', in D. Coole and S. Frost (eds), *New Materialisms: Ontology, Agency and Politics*, London: Duke University Press, pp. 1–43.

Cooper, R. (2003) *The Breaking of Nations: Order and Chaos in the Twenty-first Century*, London: Atlantic Books.

Cortell, A. P. and J. W. Davis (2000) 'Understanding the domestic impact of international norms: a research agenda', *International Studies Review*, 2(1): 65–87.

Cudworth, E. and S. Hobden (2011) *Posthuman International Relations: Complexity, Ecologism and Global Politics*, London: Zed Books.

Curtis, P. (2011) '"Nudge unit" not guaranteed to work, says Oliver Letwin', *Guardian*, 20 February.

Dallmayr, F. (2010) *The Promise of Democracy*, Albany, NY: State University of New York.

Davis, L. E. and D. C. North (1971) *Institutional Change and American Economic Growth*, Cambridge: Cambridge University Press.

Day, E. (2011) 'Julia Neuberger: "A nudge in the right direction won't run the big society"', *Observer*, 17 July.

Dean, M. (2010) *Governmentality: Power and Rule in Modern Society*, 2nd edn, London: Sage.

— (2011) 'Resisting the irresistible event', Paper presented at the Centre for Citizenship, Identities and Governance workshop 'Resisting (in) security, securing resistance', Open University, London, 12 July.

Deng, F. et al. (1996) *Sovereignty as Responsibility: Conflict Management in Africa*, Washington, DC: Brookings Institution.

Dillon, M. and J. Reid (2009) *The Liberal Way of War: Killing to Make Life Live*, London: Routledge.

Donnelly, J. (1998) *International Human Rights*, Boulder, CO: Westview Press.

Duffield, M. (2007) *Development, Security and Unending War: Governing the World of Peoples*, Cambridge: Polity.

— (2011) 'Liberal interventionism and the crisis of acceptance: from protection to resilience'. Annual Lecture, Centre for the Study of Global Security and Development, Queen Mary, University of London, 19 May.

Edwards, C. (2009) *Resilient Nation*, London: Demos, www.demos.co.uk/files/Resilient_Nation_-_web-1.pdf?1242207746.

Emerson, R. W. (1993) 'History', in R. W. Emerson, *Self-Reliance and Other Essays*, New York: Dover Publications, pp. 1–17.

Engels, F. (1947) *Anti-Dühring: Herr Eugen Dühring's Revolution in Science*, Moscow: Progress Publishers, www.marxists.org/archive/marx/works/1877/anti-duhring/.

Evans, G. (2008) *The Responsibility to Protect: Ending Mass Atrocity Crimes Once and for All*, Washington, DC: Brookings Institution.

— (2011) 'No-fly zone will help stop Gaddafi's carnage', *Financial Times*, 28 February, www.gevans.org/opeds/oped108.html.

Fine, K. (1996) 'Fragile stability and change: understanding conflict during the transitions in east central Europe', in A. Chayes and A. H. Chayes (eds), *Preventing Conflict in the Post-Communist World*, Washington, DC: Brookings Institution, pp. 541–81.

Finnemore, M. (1996a) 'Norms, culture and world politics: insights from sociology's institutionalism (a review essay)', *International Organization*, 50(2): 325–47.

— (1996b) 'Constructing norms of humanitarian intervention', in P. Katzenstein (ed.), *The Culture of National Security: Norms and Identity in World Politics*, New York: Columbia University Press, pp. 153–85.

Finnemore, M. and K. Sikkink (1998) 'International norm dynamics and political change', *International Organization*, 52(4): 887–917.

Forest, J. and C. Mehier (2001) 'John R. Commons and Herbert A. Simon on the concept of rationality', *Journal of Economic Issues*, 35(3): 591–605.

Foucault, M. (1982) 'Afterword: the subject and power', in H. L. Dreyfus and P. Rabinow, *Michel Foucault: Beyond Structuralism and Hermeneutics*, Hemel Hempstead: Harvester Wheatsheaf, pp. 208–26

— (1984) 'What is enlightenment?', in P. Rabinow (ed.), *The Foucault Reader*, New York: Pantheon Books, pp. 32–50.

— (2000a) 'Truth and juridical forms', in *Power: Essential Works of Foucault 1954–1984*, London: Penguin.

— (2000b) 'Truth and power', in *Power: Essential Works of Foucault 1954–1984*, London: Penguin, pp. 111–33.

— (2002) *The Order of Things*, London: Routledge.

— (2003) *Society Must be Defended: Lectures at the Collège de France 1975–1976*, London: Allen Lane.

— (2007) *Security, Territory and Population: Lectures at the Collège de France 1977–1978*, Basingstoke: Palgrave.

— (2008) *The Birth of Biopolitics: Lectures at the Collège de France 1978–1979*, Basingstoke: Palgrave.

— (2010) *The Government of the Self and Others: Lectures at the Collège de France 1982–1983*, Basingstoke: Palgrave.

Frost, S. (2010) 'Fear and the illusion of autonomy', in D. Coole and S. Frost (eds), *New Materialisms: Ontology, Agency and Politics*, London: Duke University Press, pp. 158–77.

Fukuyama, F. (1995) 'The primacy of culture', *Journal of Democracy*, 6(1): 7–14.

Furedi, F. (2007) *Invitation to Terror: The Expanding Empire of the Unknown*, London: Continuum.

Gandhi, M. (1931) *The Quotations Page*, 3553, www.quotationspage.com/quote/3553.html.

Ghani, A. and C. Lockhart (2008) *Fixing Failed States: A Framework for Rebuilding a Fractured World*, Oxford: Oxford University Press.

Ghani, A., C. Lockhart and M. Carnahan (2005) 'Closing the sovereignty gap: an approach to state-building', Overseas Development Institute Working Paper no. 253, ODI, September, www.odi.org.uk/publications/working_papers/wp253.pdf.

Giddens, A. (1984) *The Constitution of Society: Outline of the Theory of Structuration*, Cambridge: Polity.

— (1994) *Beyond Left and Right: The Future of Radical Politics*, Cambridge: Polity.

— (1998) *The Third Way: The Renewal of Social Democracy*, Cambridge: Polity.

— (2000) *The Third Way and Its Critics*, Cambridge: Polity.

Gillott, J. and M. Kumar (1995) *Science and the Retreat from Reason*, London: Merlin Press.

Gordon, C. (1991) 'Introduction', in G. Burchell, C. Gordon and P. Miller (eds), *The Foucault Effect: Studies in Governmental Rationality*, London: Harvester Wheatsheaf, pp. 1–51.

Graham, G. (2002) *The Case against the Democratic State*, Thorverton: Imprint Academic.

Grist, M. (2009) *Changing the Subject: How new ways of thinking about human behaviour might change politics, policy and practice*, London: RSA.

— (2010) *STEER: Mastering our behaviour through instinct, environment and reason*, London: RSA.

Gunther, R. et al. (1996) 'Debate: democratic consolidation: O'Donnell's "Illusions": a rejoinder', *Journal of Democracy*, 7(4): 151–9.

Habermas, J. (1996) *The Divided West*, Cambridge: Polity.

— (1997) *Between Facts and Norms: Contributions to a Discourse Theory of Law and Democracy*, Cambridge: Polity.

— (1999) 'Bestialität und Humanität', *Die Zeit*, 54: 1–8, trans. Franz Solms-Laubach, www.theglobalsite.ac.uk/press/011habermas.htm.

Hall, S. (2007) 'The West and the Rest: discourse and power', in T. Das Gupta et al. (eds), *Race and Racialization: Essential Readings*, Toronto: Canadian Scholars' Press, pp. 56–63.

Harman, G. (2010) *Towards Speculative Realism: Essays and Lectures*, Winchester: Zero Books.

Harrison, E. (2004) 'State socialization, international norm dynamics and the liberal peace', *International Politics*, 41(4): 521–42.

Harvey, D. (2005) *A Brief History of Neoliberalism*, Oxford: Oxford University Press.

Hawksley, H. (2009) *Democracy Kills: What's So Good about Having the Vote?*, London: Pan Macmillan.

Hay, C. (2006) 'Constructivist institutionalism', in R. A. W. Rhodes, S. A. Binder and B. A. Rockman (eds), *The Oxford Handbook of Political Institutions*, Oxford: Oxford University Press, pp. 56–74.

Hayek, F. (1952) *The Sensory Order: An Inquiry into the Foundations of Theoretical Psychology*, Chicago, IL: University of Chicago Press.

— (1960) *The Constitution of Liberty*, London: Routledge.

Held, D. (1995) *Democracy and the Global Order*, Cambridge: Polity.

HMG (2012) *Social Justice: Transforming Lives*, London: HM Government, www.dwp.gov.uk/docs/social-justice-transforming-lives.pdf.

Hollis, M. and S. Smith (1990) *Explaining and Understanding International Relations*, Oxford: Clarendon Press.

Hopgood, S. (2000) 'Reading the small print in global civil society: the inexorable hegemony of the liberal self', *Millennium: Journal of International Studies*, 29(1): 1–25.

ICISS (2001a) *The Responsibility to Protect: Report of the International Commission on Intervention and State Sovereignty*, Ottawa: International Development Research Centre.

— (2001b) *The Responsibility to Protect: Research, Bibliography, Background*, Ottawa: International Development Research Centre.

IfG (Institute for Government) (2010) *Mindspace: Influencing behaviour through public policy: the practical guide*, London: Cabinet Office.

Ilyenkov, E. V. (1982) *Leninist Dialectics and the Metaphysics of Positivism: Reflections on V. I. Lenin's book 'Materialism and Empirio-Criticism'*, London: New Park Publications.

Jackson, R. H. and G. Sorensen (2010) *Introduction to International Relations: Theories and Approaches*, Oxford: Oxford University Press.

Jepperson, R. L., A. Wendt and P. Katzenstein (1996) 'Norms, identity, and culture in national security', in P. J. Katzenstein (ed.), *The Culture of National Security: Norms and Identity in World Politics*, New York: Columbia University Press, pp. 33–75.

Jervis, R. and J. Snyder (eds) (1991) *Dominoes and Bandwagons: Strategic*

Beliefs and Great Power Competition in the Eurasian Rimland, Oxford: Oxford University Press.

Joerges, C. (2010) 'Unity in diversity as Europe's vocation and conflicts law as Europe's constitutional form', LSE 'Europe in question' Discussion Paper Series 28, December.

John, P. et al. (2011) *Nudge, Nudge, Think, Think: Experimenting with Ways to Change Civic Behaviour*, London: Bloomsbury.

Joseph, J. (2012) *The Social in the Global: Social Theory, Governmentality and Global Politics*, Cambridge: Cambridge University Press.

Kaldor, M. (1999) *New and Old Wars: Organized Violence in a Global Era*, Cambridge: Polity.

— (2003) *Global Civil Society: An Answer to War*, Cambridge: Polity.

— (2007) *Human Security: Reflections on Globalization and Intervention*, Cambridge: Polity.

— (2011) 'Libya: war or humanitarian intervention?', *Open Democracy*, 29 March, www.opendemocracy. net/mary-kaldor/libya-war-or-humanitarian-intervention.

Kant, I. (1970) 'On the common saying: "This may be true in theory, but it does not apply in practice"', in *Kant: Political Writings*, Cambridge: Cambridge University Press.

— (1999) *Metaphysical Elements of Justice*, 2nd edn, Indianapolis, IN: Hackett Publishing.

Katzenstein, P. J. (1996a) 'Introduction: Alternative perspectives on national security', in P. J. Katzenstein (ed.), *The Culture of National Security: Norms and Identity in World Politics*, New York: Columbia University Press, pp. 1–32.

— (1996b) 'Conclusion: National security in a changing world', in P. J. Katzenstein (ed.), *The Culture of National Security: Norms and Identity*

in World Politics, New York: Columbia University Press, pp. 498–537.

Katzenstein, P. J., R. O. Keohane and S. D. Krasner (1998) '*International Organization* and the study of world politics', *International Organization*, 52(4): 645–85.

Kauffman, S. (1995) *At Home in the Universe: The Search for Laws of Self Organization and Complexity*, Oxford: Oxford University Press.

Keane, J. (2003) *Global Civil Society?*, Cambridge: Cambridge University Press.

Keck, M. E. and K. Sikkink (1998) *Activists beyond Borders: Advocacy Networks in International Politics*, Ithaca, NY: Cornell University Press.

Keohane, R. O. (1988) 'International institutions: two approaches', *International Studies Quarterly*, 32(4): 379–96.

— (1989) *International Institutions and State Power*, Boulder, CO: Westview Press.

Kottow, M. H. (2002) 'The vulnerable and the susceptible', *Bioethics*, 17: 5–6, 460–71.

Kowert, P. and J. Legro (1996) 'Norms, identity, and their limits: a theoretical reprise', in P. J. Katzenstein (ed.), *The Culture of National Security: Norms and Identity in World Politics*, New York: Columbia University Press, pp. 451–97.

Krasner, S. D. (ed.) (1983) *International Regimes*, Ithaca, NY: Cornell University Press.

— (2004) 'Sharing sovereignty: new institutions for collapsing and failing states', *International Security*, 29(2): 5–43.

— (2005) 'The case for shared sovereignty', *Journal of Democracy*, 16(1): 69–83.

Kratochwil, F. (2000) 'Constructing a new orthodoxy? Wendt's social theory of international politics and the constructivist challenge', *Millennium: Journal of International Studies*, 29(1): 73–101.

Krish, N. (2002) 'Review essay: legality, morality and the dilemma of international intervention after Kosovo', *European Journal of International Law*, 13(1): 323–35.

Laïdi, Z. (2008) 'European preferences and their reception', in Z. Laïdi (ed.), *EU Foreign Policy in a Globalized World: Normative Power and Social Preferences*, London: Routledge, pp. 1–20.

Latour, B. (1993) *We Have Never been Modern*, Cambridge, MA: Harvard University Press.

Lenin, V. I. (1972) 'Materialism and empirio-criticism: critical comments on a reactionary philosophy', in V. I. Lenin, *Collected Works*, 14, Moscow: Progress Publishers, pp. 17–362, www.marxists.org/archive/lenin/works/1908/mec/.

Lentzos, F. and N. Rose (2009) 'Governing insecurity: contingency planning, protection, resilience', *Economy and Society*, 38(2): 230–54.

Linklater, A. (1998) *The Transformation of Political Community*, Cambridge: Polity.

Lugard, Lord (1923) *The Dual Mandate in British Tropical Africa*, Abingdon: Frank Cass.

Mac Ginty, R. (2011) *International Peacebuilding and Local Resistance: Hybrid Forms of Peace*, Basingstoke: Palgrave.

Macdonald, D. J. (1995) 'Communist bloc expansion in the early Cold War: challenging realism, refuting revisionism', *International Security*, 20(3): 152–88.

Mack, A. (2004) 'A signifier of shared values', *Security Dialogue*, 35(3): 366–7.

Macpherson, C. B. (1962) *The Political Theory of Possessive Individualism: Hobbes to Locke*, Oxford: Oxford University Press.

Mahoney, J. and K. Thelen (eds) (2010) *Explaining Institutional Change: Ambiguity, Agency, and Power*, Cambridge: Cambridge University Press.

Martin, M. and T. Owen (2010) 'The second generation of human security: lessons from the UN and EU experience', *International Affairs*, 86(1): 212–24.

Martinsson, J. (2011) *Global Norms: Creation, Diffusion, and Limits*, World Bank/Communication for Governance and Accountability Program, siteresources.worldbank.org/EXTGOVACC/Resources/Final-GlobalNormsv1.pdf.

Marx, K. (1852) *The Eighteenth Brumaire of Louis Bonaparte*, www.marxists.org/archive/marx/works/1852/18th-brumaire/.

— (1954) *Capital*, vol. 1, London: Lawrence and Wishart.

— (n.d.) 'The Trinity Formula', *Capital*, vol. 3, ch. 48, www.marxists.org/archive/marx/works/1894-c3/ch48.htm.

Marx, K. and F. Engels (1970) *The German Ideology*, London: Lawrence & Wishart.

Masten, A. S. and J. L. Powell (2003) 'A resilience framework for research, policy and practice', in S. S. Luthar (ed.), *Resilience and Vulnerability: Adaptation in the Context of Childhood Adversities*, Cambridge: Cambridge University Press, pp. 1–27.

McFaul, M. A. (2004) 'Democracy promotion as a world value', *Washington Quarterly*, 28(1): 147–63.

Miller, P. and N. Rose (2008) *Governing the Present: Administering Economic, Social and Personal Life*, Cambridge: Polity.

Nakamura, J. and M. Csikszentmihalyi (2009) 'Flow theory and research', in C. R. Snyder and S. J. Lopez (eds),

Oxford Handbook of Positive Psychology, 2nd edn, Oxford: Oxford University Press, pp. 195–206.

Navarro, V. (2000) 'Development and quality of life: a critique of Amartya Sen's Development as Freedom', *International Journal of Health Services: Planning, Administration and Evaluation*, 30(4): 661–74.

Neenan, M. (2009) *Developing Resilience: A Cognitive Behavioural Approach*, London: Routledge.

Newman, E., R. Paris and O. P. Richmond (eds) (2009) *New Perspectives on Liberal Peacebuilding*, New York: United Nations University Press.

Nietzsche, F. W. (1984) *Human, All Too Human*, London: Penguin Books.

— (1997) *Beyond Good and Evil: Prelude to a Philosophy of the Future*, New York: Dover Publications.

— (2006) *The Gay Science*, New York: Dover Publications.

— (2007a) *The Twilight of the Idols*, Ware, Hertfordshire: Wordsworth Classics of World Literature.

— (2007b) 'The Antichrist', in F. Nietzsche, *The Twilight of the Idols*, Ware, Hertfordshire: Wordsworth Classics of World Literature, pp. 91–163.

North, D. C. (1990) *Institutions, Institutional Change and Economic Performance*, Cambridge: Cambridge University Press.

— (2005) *Understanding the Process of Economic Change*, Princeton, NJ: Princeton University Press.

North, D. C. and R. P. Thomas (1973) *The Rise of the Western World*, Cambridge: Cambridge University Press.

North, D. C., J. J. Wallis and B. R. Weingast (2009) *Violence and Social Orders: A Conceptual Framework for Interpreting Recorded Human History*, Cambridge: Cambridge University Press.

NSS (2002) *National Security Strategy of the United States of America*, www.au.af.mil/au/awc/awcgate/nss/nss_sep2002.pdf.

Nussbaum, M. C. (2011) *Creating Capabilities: The Human Development Approach*, Cambridge, MA: Harvard University Press.

O'Donnell, G. (1996) 'Illusions about consolidation', *Journal of Democracy*, 7(2): 34–51.

Ogata, S. (n.d.) 'Empowering people for human security', Presentation at the 56th Annual DPI/NGO Conference, www.google.co.uk/url?sa=t&source=web&cd=1&sqi=2&ved=0CCUQFjAA&url=http%3A%2F%2Fochaonline.un.org%2FOchaLinkClick.aspx%3Flink%3Docha%26docId%3D1087393&rct=j&q=human%20security%20empwerment&ei=0Mn7TZrPK8KEhQea_JmvAw&usg=AFQjCNHx-2KUo2ohpplwnEWwkUGS6xuXwQ.

O'Malley, P. (2004) *Risk, Uncertainty and Government*, London: Routledge.

— (2010) 'Resilient subjects: uncertainty, warfare and liberalism', *Economy and Society*, 29(4): 488–509.

Orford, A. (2011) *International Authority and the Responsibility to Protect*, Cambridge: Cambridge University Press.

Owens, P. (2012) 'Human security and the rise of the social', *Review of International Studies*, 38(3): 547–67.

Paffenholz, T. (2009) *Civil Society and Peacebuilding: A Critical Assessment*, Boulder, CO: Lynne Rienner.

Palan, R. (2000) 'A world of their making: an evaluation of the constructivist critique in international relations', *Review of International Studies*, 26(4): 575–98.

Parekh, B. (2000) *Rethinking Multiculturalism: Cultural Diversity and Political Theory*, Basingstoke: Macmillan.

Paris, R. (2004a) *At War's End: Building Peace after Conflict*, Cambridge: Cambridge University Press.

— (2004b) 'Still an inscrutable concept', *Security Dialogue*, 35(3): 370–2.

Paris, R. and T. D. Sisk (eds) (2009) *The Dilemmas of Statebuilding: Confronting the Contradictions of Postwar Peace Operations*, London: Routledge.

Parkin, D. M. (2011) 'The fraction of cancer attributable to lifestyle and environmental factors in the UK in 2010', *British Journal of Cancer*, 105: S2–S5, www.nature.com/bjc/journal/v105/n2s/pdf/bjc2011474a.pdf.

Pender, J. (2001) 'From "structural adjustment" to "comprehensive development framework": conditionality transformed?', *Third World Quarterly*, 22(3): 397–411.

Peters, B. G. (2005) *Institutional Theory in Political Science: The 'New Institutionalism'*, 2nd edn, London: Continuum.

Plato (1960) *Georgias*, London: Penguin.

— (n.d.) 'Book II', in Plato, *The Republic*, trans. Benjamin Jowett, classics.mit.edu/Plato/republic.3.ii.html.

Polit, D. F. and C. T. Beck (2004) *Nursing Research: Principles and Methods*, Philadelphia, PA: Lippincott, Williams & Wilkins.

Powell, W. W. and P. J. DiMaggio (1991) *New Institutionalism in Organizational Analysis*, Chicago, IL: Chicago University Press.

Prigogine, I. (2003) *Is Future Given?*, New York: Bantam.

Pupavac, V. (2007) 'Witnessing the demise of the developing state: problems for humanitarian advocacy', in A. Hehir and N. Robinson (eds), *State-building: Theory and Practice*, London: Routledge.

Reivich, K. and A. Shatte (2003) *The Resilience Factor: 7 Keys to Finding Your Inner Strength and Overcoming Life's Hurdles*, New York: Broadway Books.

Reus-Smit, C. (2001) 'Constructivism', in S. Burchill et al., *Theories of International Relations*, Basingstoke: Palgrave, pp. 209–30.

Richards, D. and M. Smith (2011) 'Good governance and civil service reform', Written evidence submitted to the UK Parliament Public Administration Select Committee, 2010/11 session, www.publications.parliament.uk/pa/cm201011/cmselect/cmpubadm/writev/goodgov/gg14.htm.

Richmond, O. P. (2005) *The Transformation of Peace*, Basingstoke: Palgrave.

— (2010) 'Resistance and the post-liberal peace', *Millennium: Journal of International Studies*, 38(3): 665–92.

— (2011) *A Post-Liberal Peace: The Infrapolitics of Peacebuilding*, London: Routledge.

Richmond, O. P. and J. Franks (2009) *Liberal Peace Transitions: Between Statebuilding and Peacebuilding*, Edinburgh: Edinburgh University Press.

Risse, T. and S. C. Ropp (1999) 'International human rights norms and domestic change: conclusions', in T. Risse, S. C. Ropp and K. Sikkink, *The Power of Human Rights: International Norms and Domestic Change*, Cambridge: Cambridge University Press, pp. 234–78.

Risse, T. and K. Sikkink (1999) 'The socialization of international human rights norms into domestic practices: introduction', in T. Risse, S. C. Ropp and K. Sikkink (eds), *The Power of Human Rights: International Norms and Domestic Change*, Cambridge: Cambridge University Press, pp. 1–38.

Risse, T., S. C. Ropp and K. Sikkink (eds) (1999) *The Power of Human Rights: International Norms and Domestic Change*, Cambridge: Cambridge University Press.

Risse-Kappen, T. (1994) 'Ideas do not float freely: transnational coalitions, domestic structures, and the end of the Cold War', *International Organization*, 48(2): 185–214.

— (ed.) (1995) *Bringing Transnational Relations Back In: Non-State Actors, Domestic Structures, and International Institutions*, Cambridge: Cambridge University Press.

Roberts, D. (2008) 'Hybrid polities and indigenous pluralities: advanced lessons in statebuilding from Cambodia', *Journal of Intervention and Statebuilding*, 2(1): 63–86.

— (2009) *Global Governance and Biopolitics: Regulating Human Security*, London: Zed Books.

Roberts, M. (2011) 'Over 40% of cancers due to lifestyle: says review', *BBC News*, 7 December, www.bbc.co.uk/news/health-16031149.

Robertson, G. (1999) *Crimes against Humanity: The Struggle for Global Justice*, London: Allen Lane.

— (2011) 'How the West can end Gaddafi's slaughter', *Sydney Morning Herald*, 7 March, www.smh.com.au/opinion/politics/how-the-west-can-end-gaddafis-slaughter-20110306-1bjgs.html.

Rose, N. (1989) *Governing the Soul: The Shaping of the Private Self*, London: Free Association Books.

— (1999) *Powers of Freedom: Reframing Political Thought*, Cambridge: Cambridge University Press.

Rumsfeld, D. (2002) 'United States Department of Defence news briefing – Secretary Rumsfeld and Gen. Myers', 12 February, www.defense.gov/transcripts/transcript.aspx?transcriptid=2636.

Said, E. (1995) *Orientalism: Western Conceptions of the Orient*, London: Penguin.

Saint-Paul, G. (2011) *The Tyranny of Utility: Behavioural Social Science and the Rise of Paternalism*, Princeton, NJ: Princeton University Press.

Samaddar, R. (2006) *Flags and Rights*, Kolkata: Mahanirban Calcutta Research Group.

Schmitt, C. (2003) *The Nomos of the Earth: In the International Law of the Jus Publicum Europaeum*, New York: Telos.

Schmitter, P. C. and T. L. Karl (1991) 'What democracy is ... and is not', *Journal of Democracy*, 2(3): 4–17.

Scott, W. R. (2008) *Institutions and Organizations: Ideas and Interests*, 3rd edn, London: Sage.

Sen, A. (1987) *On Ethics and Economics*, Oxford: Blackwell.

— (1992) *Inequality Reexamined*, Oxford: Oxford University Press.

— (1997) 'Human rights and Asian values', *New Republic*, 14–21 July.

— (1999) *Development as Freedom*, Oxford: Oxford University Press.

— (2006) *Identity and Violence: The Illusion of Destiny*, London: Penguin.

— (2009) *The Idea of Justice*, London: Allen Lane.

Sewer, D. (2011) 'The strikes on Libya: humanitarian intervention, not imperial aggression', *The Atlantic*, 19 March, www.theatlantic.com/international/archive/2011/03/the-strikes-on-libya-humanitarian-intervention-not-imperial-aggression/72740/.

Snyder, J. (2000) *From Voting to Violence: Democratization and Nationalist Conflict*, New York: W. W. Norton.

Steinmo, S., K. Thelen and F. Longstreth (eds) (1992) *Structuring Politics: Historical Institutionalism in Comparative Analysis*, Cambridge: Cambridge University Press.

Stengers, I. (2011) *Cosmopolitics II*, Minneapolis: University of Minnesota Press.

Tadjbakhsh, S. (ed.) (2011) *Rethinking the Liberal Peace: External Models and Local Alternatives*, London: Routledge.

Tadjbakhsh, S. and A. M. Chenoy (2007) *Human Security: Concepts and Implications*, London: Routledge.

Thaler, R. H. and C. R. Sunstein (2008) *Nudge: Improving Decisions about Health, Wealth and Happiness*, London: Penguin.

Thomas, C. (2004) 'A bridge between the interconnected challenges confronting the world', *Security Dialogue*, 35(3): 353–4.

Thomas, D. C. (2001) *The Helsinki Effect: International Norms, Human Rights, and the Demise of Communism*, Princeton, NJ: Princeton University Press.

— (2011) *Making EU Foreign Policy: National Preferences, European Norms and Common Policies*, London: Palgrave Macmillan.

Todorova, M. (1997) *Imagining the Balkans*, New York: Oxford University Press.

Touraine, A. (1977) *The Self-Production of Society*, Chicago, IL: University of Chicago Press.

UK Cabinet Office (2011a) *UK Resilience*, www.cabinetoffice.gov.uk/uk resilience.

— (2011b) *Strategic National Framework on Community Resilience*, March, www.cabinetoffice.gov.uk/sites/ default/files/resources/Strategic-National-Framework-on-Community-Resilience_0.pdf.

UNDP (1990) *Human Development Report 1990: The Concept and Measurement of Human Development*, New York: United Nations Development Programme.

— (1994) *Human Development Report 1994: New Dimensions of Human Security*, New York: UNDP, hdr.undp. org/en/reports/global/hdr1994/ chapters/

UNSG (2009) *Implementing the Responsibility to Protect: Report of the Secretary-General*, 12 January, A/63/677, globalr2p.org/pdf/ SGR2PEng.pdf

— (2010) *Human Security: Report of the Secretary-General, 8 March*, A/64/701, responsibilitytoprotect.org/Human %20Security%20Report%20 2010. pdf.

Urry, J. (2003) *Global Complexity*, Cambridge: Polity.

Walker, B. and D. Salt (2006) *Resilience Thinking: Sustaining Ecosystems and People in a Changing World*, Washington, DC: Island Press.

Walker, J. and M. Cooper (2011) 'Genealogies of resilience: from systems ecology to the political economy of crisis adaptation', *Security Dialogue*, 42(2): 143–60.

Watson, S. (2011) 'The "human" as referent object?: Humanitarianism as securitization', *Security Dialogue*, 42(1): 3–20.

Weldes, J., M. Laffey, H. Gusterson and R. Duvall (eds) (1999) *Cultures of Insecurity: States, Communities, and the Production of Danger*, Minneapolis: University of Minnesota Press.

Wendt, A. (1992) 'Anarchy is what states make of it: the social construction of power politics', *International Organization*, 46(2): 391–425.

— (1999) *Social Theory of International Politics*, Cambridge: Cambridge University Press.

Widmaier, W. (2011) 'Taking stock of norms research – from structural, cognitive and psychological constructivisms to intellectual irony and populist paradox', Participant write-up, IPS working group on 'Norms', International Studies Association, Annual Convention 2011, Montreal, 15–19 March, www.isanet.org/ isa_working_groups_ips/2011/03/ ips-working-group-widmaier-write-up.html.

Wight, C. (2006) *Agents, Structures and International Relations: Politics as Ontology*, Cambridge: Cambridge University Press.

Wolff, L. (1994) *Inventing Eastern Europe:*

The Map of Civilization on the Mind of the Enlightenment, Stanford, CA: Stanford University Press.

World Bank (1997) *World Development Report 1997: The State in a Changing World*, Washington, DC: IBRD/World Bank.

— (2000) *Reforming Public Institutions and Strengthening Governance: A World Bank Strategy*, Washington, DC: IBRD/World Bank.

— (2006) *World Development Report 2007: Development and the Next Generation*, Washington, DC: World Bank.

WRI (2008) *World Resources 2008: Roots of Resilience – Growing the Wealth of the Poor*, Washington, DC: World Resources Institute.

Youngs, R. (2002) *The European Union and the Promotion of Democracy: Europe's Mediterranean and Asian Policies*, Oxford: Oxford University Press.

Zakharia, F. (2003) *The Future of Freedom; Illiberal Democracy at Home and Abroad*, New York: W. W. Norton.

Zanotti, L. (2006) 'International security, normalization and Croatia's Euro-Atlantic integration', European University Institute Working Papers, SPS no. 2006/02.

— (2011) *Governing Disorder: UN Peace Operations, International Security, and Democratization in the Post-Cold War Era*, University Park, PA: Pennsylvania State University Press.

Zaum, D. (2007) *The Sovereignty Paradox: The Norms and Politics of International Statebuilding*, Oxford: Oxford University Press.

INDEX